KU-717-391

WITHDRAWN
FROM STOCK

WITHDRAWN
FROM STOCK

POLITICAL THINKERS
edited by Geraint Parry
University of Glasgow

4
JOHN STUART MILL

POLITICAL THINKERS

JOHN STUART MILL

R. J. Halliday
Senior Lecturer in Politics
at the University of Warwick

WITHDRAWN FROM STOCK

London
George Allen & Unwin Ltd
Ruskin House   Museum Street

First published in 1976

This book is copyright under the Berne Convention. All
rights are reserved. Apart from any fair dealing for the
purpose of private study, research, criticism or review, as
permitted under the Copyright Act, 1956, no part of this
publication may be reproduced, stored in a retrieval system,
or transmitted, in any form or by any means, electronic,
electrical, chemical, mechanical, optical, photocopying,
recording or otherwise, without the prior permission of the
copyright owner. Enquiries should be addressed to the
publishers.

© George Allen & Unwin (Publishers) Ltd 1976

ISBN 0 04 320113 x hardback
0 04 320114 8 paperback

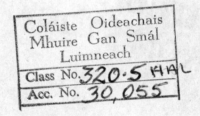

Coláiste Oideachais
Mhuire Gan Smál
Luimneach

Class No. 320.5 HAL
Acc. No. 30,055

Printed in Great Britain
in 10 point Plantin type
by Butler & Tanner Ltd
Frome and London

To
Sondra
Karen
and
Fiona

PREFACE

This book offers an introduction to the political thinking of John Stuart Mill, a deeply pessimistic and humourless man, with conflicting commitments borrowed from many different sources. As an introduction, it can do little more than point towards these, indicating the most important ones here and there. The introductory format may also tend to suggest rather more coherence and clarity than actually exists in Mill's writings. This is not necessarily a bad thing. Ever since his death in 1873, commentators and critics have been busy sniffing out contradictions and hunting down paradoxes. No one doubts that this has been very valuable; quite rightly, political theorists have become suspicious of those who think and write badly. But there is always coherence as well as incoherence, success as well as failure, and the commentator should always set one in the context of the other. Only the reader can judge whether this has been done adequately in this case. At least I have tried to avoid the enormous condescension which runs through so many recent interpretations of Mill.

Four people have been particularly helpful in the production of this book. Miss Jean Fife was all that a typist ought to be. Professor Wilfrid Harrison and Dr Peter Burnell, colleagues in the Department of Politics, read the whole of the typescript with great care and consideration. Their comments were always helpful. Professor Geraint Parry, the editor of this series and a former colleague, showed the two prime virtues of all good editors—patience and efficiency. My grateful thanks go to them all. Obviously, they are not to blame for whatever defects and mistakes remain.

Coventry, August 1975

CONTENTS

A CHRONOLOGY

1806   Born 20 May in London, the eldest son of James Mill.

1809–20   Educated at home by his father, beginning Greek at the age
          of 3, Latin at the age of 8 and chemistry before the age of 12.

1821–2   Studies Roman Law with John Austin and begins to write
          for newspapers. Reads Bentham for the first time and is
          converted to Benthamism by reading Dumont's French
          edition of his writings. Immediately begins to be active in
          radical causes.

1823   Starts employment as a clerk at India House in the office of
          the Examiner of India Correspondence. Arrested but not
          imprisoned for distributing birth-control propaganda.

1825   Edits Bentham's *Rationale of Judicial Evidence* in five
          volumes and helps to found the London Debating Society.

1826–7   The mental crisis.

1828   Promoted at India House and establishes contacts with
          Saint-Simonians and Coleridgeans at the London Debating
          Society. Forms close personal friendship with John Sterling.

1829   Alienates many radical friends by his defence of Words-
          worth at the London Debating Society. Reads Comte for
          the first time.

1830   Visits Paris and begins to write extensively on France and
          French affairs, particularly for the *Examiner*. Meets and
          becomes infatuated with Harriet Taylor.

1831–2   Publishes 'The Spirit of the Age', reviews the poems of
          Tennyson and writes *Essays on Some Unsettled Questions
          of Political Economy*. Visits Wordsworth in the Lakes and
          begins to write on the main problems in logic.

1833   Publishes several essays and reviews on poetry and con-
          tributes an anonymous critique of Bentham's philosophy
          to Lytton Bulwer's *England and the English*.

1835   Rediscovers an interest in radicalism. Founds and edits
          the *London and Westminster Review* and reads and reviews
          Tocqueville on America.

1836   Severe illness following the death of his father. Travels in
          Europe and is promoted at India House.

1838   Completes his article the 'Reorganization of the Reform
          Party' and publishes his essay on 'Bentham'. Continues to
          work and to write on the main problems in logic.

1840   Publishes essay on 'Coleridge' and gives up proprietorship
          of the *London and Westminster Review*. Reads and reviews
          the second volume of Tocqueville on America.

1841   Rewrites the drafts of his book on logic, offers it for publica-
          tion and is turned down.

1843 Publishes *A System of Logic* and reviews Michelet's *History of France*.

1844–5 Publishes *Essays on Some Unsettled Questions of Political Economy* and begins his critique of paternalism by publishing 'The Claims of Labour'. In the autumn of 1845 begins writing *Principles of Political Economy*.

1848 Publishes *Principles of Political Economy* and defends the revolutions in Europe against the parties of order in several articles.

1851 Marries Harriet Taylor.

1854 Severe illness. Mill travels extensively in Greece and Italy, deciding to convert an essay written in 1854 into a volume on liberty. Also continues writing the *Autobiography*.

1856 Promoted to Chief Examiner of India Correspondence, position his father had held.

1858 Parliament takes over the administration of India. Mill refuses offer of post in government and retires from India House. Harriet Taylor dies in Avignon.

1859 Publishes *On Liberty, Dissertations and Discussions*, volumes one and two, and *Thoughts on Parliamentary Reform*. From now on Mill spends about half of each year in Avignon.

1861 The essays *Representative Government* and *Utilitarianism* published, the latter as magazine articles. Revises the *Autobiography*.

1862 Publishes *Utilitarianism* as a book and reviews Austin on jurisprudence.

1865 Elected MP for the Westminster constituency, publishes *An Examination of Sir William Hamilton's Philosophy* and *Auguste Comte and Positivism*.

1867 Proposes the Hare plan as an amendment to the Representation of the People Bill and also fails in an attempt to gain the vote for women. Publishes *Dissertations and Discussions*, volume three.

1868 Fails to be re-elected for Westminster, largely due to his activities against Governor Eyre on the Jamaica Committee.

1869 Publishes *Subjection of Women* and produces an annotated edition of James Mill's *Analysis of the Phenomena of the Human Mind*. Undertakes final revision of the *Autobiography*.

1870 Publishes writings on the Irish land question and finally completes the revision of the *Autobiography*.

1873 Dies 7 May at Avignon.

The Mental Crisis

The months and years immediately following the mental and emotional crisis which began in the autumn and winter of 1826 were a time of permanent revolution in Mill's thinking. He was involved in a complex and painful renunciation of his early beliefs. The four years of confident political activism which had resulted from his final conversion to Benthamism in 1822 were now over. There was no question of his making minor modifications to his views; the changes were wholesale and drastic. We can reject straight away, then, any interpretation which would present the crisis and its resolution as either insignificant or inconsequential. This would plainly be false. No doubt the *Autobiography* gives an ambiguous, almost confused account of the crisis.[1] It was begun almost thirty years after the event, the immediate stimulus being Mill's discovery that he was suffering from consumption. Mill obviously wrote to produce an imaginative reconstruction of an experience, not to record a simple chronology of occurrences. The fallibility of memory and the partiality of retrospective judgement are only too apparent, particularly given an occasional desire to mimic the views of Harriet Taylor. There is also very little self-revelation and few intimate personal details. As a public figure with a well-established sense of his historical role, Mill had no time for that particular genre. Even the account of his love for Harriet Taylor has a disembodied, curiously impersonal air; a true reflection, perhaps, of the nature of their relationship. Some allowance might also be made for age and education. Brought up with a mixture of mollycoddling and bullying by a sour and authoritarian father, protected at one moment and exposed at another, Mill was a very young 20-year-old indeed in 1826.[2] He was, in fact, thoroughly naïve. And like many adolescents he was a persistent and well-known grumbler. He was also tired out. He had spent the eighteen months preceding the crisis as Bentham's secretary and amanuensis, combining this work for an erratic and somewhat peculiar master with the routine of his employment as a clerk at India House. All of this must be borne in mind when considering the crisis and in making use of the *Autobiography*.

13

But the crisis was far more than a temporary adolescent upset, imperfectly remembered and inadequately reported. There are certainly no grounds for minimising its importance. As well as fretting and making an emotional fuss, Mill was also consciously and carefully taking decisions. Every day and every week, he seemed to be facing choices he had never faced before. Not all of these choices were serious, of course, and some were very trivial indeed; the problems they sought to resolve lasted only a moment and were soon forgotten. But in general the choices and decisions Mill faced affected not merely petty details and peripheral issues, but his whole attitude to life. His previous conception of man and politics was falling to pieces. His faith in Benthamism was dwindling and the whole ethos of radicalism was less and less appealing. Yet he could hardly turn to his father for advice and assistance, and he had no very close friends. Almost every decision carried a weighting of personal drama and excitement because of this awkward loneliness. This may be what sustains interest in the *Autobiography*. Despite a lack of intimate detail, despite the confusions and inconsistencies, Mill was telling a dramatic story of wholesale intellectual reconstruction achieved in relative isolation. For this reason alone, we prefer to take him at his own word, at least at the outset. There was a 'crisis' in his 'mental history', not just a silly or trivial truancy from the Benthamite school, and his experiences at this time were decisive in all that he subsequently did. While his political thinking should not be regarded as simply an ideological extension or appendage of his personal biography, no interpretation can dispense with an analysis of the so-called 'mental crisis' and the consequences of Mill's commitment to self-culture.

Furthermore, if the logic of the *Autobiography* is occasionally elusive, the mood is unmistakable. These were years of urgent and restless change, when there was no certainty of the future and very little love for the past. Many influences were at work, and no one should be too confident in separating one from another. There was a lot of emotional stress. There was a quickened sense of purpose. Mill also had the benefit of new personal friendships and new sets of acquaintances; he moved for the first time, for instance in dissenting unitarian circles. He also made contact with Coleridge and with the Cambridge apostles of English idealism. Above all, perhaps, came an acquaintance with unfamiliar ideas, as well as a more complex appreciation of those with which he was already familiar. All of these influences combined to allow very little of Mill's previous Benthamism to remain untouched or unquestioned. But we should not exaggerate. A great many significant decisions were obviously being taken. There was a marked loss of faith in philosophic radicalism. Mill even felt guilt and embarrassment at his previous enthusiasms, wondering how he could possibly have acted as he did. But despite all this, there was no single and dramatic collapse and Mill's commitment to utilitarian rationalism did not vanish overnight. As always, there were many backward glances, continuity as well as discontinuity. Some of Mill's previous attitudes and ideas could be dispensed with and then replaced far more easily than others. A few were questioned only now and then. Others, like those on birth-control and population dynamics, for instance, which Mill had borrowed from Malthus and Place, remained completely set, being taken more or less for granted. Obviously, in this tangle of beliefs and attitudes one must pick one's way carefully.

We identify three significant shifts of opinion: one in analytic psychology; one in political philosophy and one in the whole disposition and emphasis of Mill's epistemology. Our first two chapters examine these shifts in some detail. The first shift led to a belief in self-culture, to the pursuit of eclecticism and ultimately to a strong desire for unanimity in moral and political speculation. Indeed, from this moment, Mill was always concerned to promote agreement by avoiding an appeal to first or final principles. He preferred, instead, to recommend secondary or intermediate maxims capable of inspiring broad agreement. It is this which gives his thinking a non-dogmatic, almost pragmatic bent. The second shift provoked a quiet and contemplative toryism. Mill acquired an enduring concern for national character, as well as a distaste for those cultures, like the English and the American, which were dominated by money-grubbing and competition for material gain. What mattered here was strong authority and noble ideals rather than the prosaic contingencies of time, place and circumstance. Occasionally, this toryism issued as an irritable and aristocratic disdain for the ordinary man. The third and final shift pulled Mill away from an analytic rationalism towards romanticism. With Coleridge and Wordsworth, as his mentors, in place of Bentham, Mill acquired distinct and almost idealist notions of mind, knowledge and truth. And although he never abandoned the habit of close and precise thinking, he was increasingly inclined to recommend a union of philosophy and poetry, to abandon positivism and to modify his associationism in order to take proper account of emotion and feeling.

However, this characterisation is still far too simple. The shifts were decisive, and they did lead far from the logic and spirit of Benthamism, but they were not neat and separate adjustments, clinically conceived and coldly executed as if to a plan. To suppose otherwise would be to assume more deliberative control than Mill exercised and rather less perplexity than he actually experienced. He could not foresee where he would end. While each of the choices made at this time set up the conditions for other choices, those choices were never made in exactly the same circumstances with precisely the same outcome. We should look at the three shifts I have mentioned as parts of an uneven and loosely fitting process of change, which come together in rather different ways at different times. There was no inevitability about these changes. One cannot mark out distinct and sequential periods in the evolution of Mill's thinking, each with an appropriate text and rationale, except perhaps as a very limited and strictly heuristic exercise.[3] The changes which shaped Mill's political thinking were accomplished piecemeal, over at least a decade. Some kind of conclusion or pause, perhaps, was reached in the middle of the 1830s when Mill rediscovered an interest in radicalism. Very little has been written about this, but Mill worked hard at that time to reorganise the radical party and to fashion an appropriate 'philosophy of movement'. Certainly his new ideas and his own variant of utilitarianism, which was now explicitly based on an ethic of self-development, were first seriously tested in public at this time. This new utilitarian philosophy is examined in Chapter II. But what really mattered in these years was not this emphasis or that, not one particular consequence rather than another, but Mill's whole mood and outlook. After the crisis, Mill threw his mind wide open. He was intent on intellectual change, and desperate to reshape his own character, to avoid emotional impoverishment and to acquire completely new attitudes. In the end, the three shifts indicated —in political philosophy, psychology and epistemology—were significant only because of this.

Another point should be made. While Mill always remained an unremitting critic of his early education and instruction, constantly regretting that he had been made into the narrow, manufactured man of the radical movement, he found it impossible to be completely ungrateful. He made this clear to Carlyle several times. 'Fortunately however I was not crammed; my own thinking faculties were called into strong though but partial play; and by their means I have been enabled to *remake* all my opinions.'[4] He felt his education had at least made it possible for him to begin again, and this was enough to give him a mild admiration for the didactic exercises of his youth. After the autumn of 1826 and the 'melancholy winter' of 1827, after some six months of misery, despair and disillusion, when Mill dragged through his usual occupations 'mechanically by mere force of habit', some enthusiasm and some confidence had indeed returned. This ambivalence towards his own education, with Mill alternating between modest praise, muted criticism and vehement condemnation, is of minor importance in interpreting Mill's political thinking. While he never in any sense retracted his early criticisms of rationalism, his own ability to survive the crisis occasionally led him to wonder whether those criticisms had been entirely fair. This was particularly so when he became convinced, as he did in the fifties, that his rejection of Benthamism had been badly timed and tactically unfortunate for the radical cause.

This ambivalence towards his own education has led several commentators to postulate a mature Mill, a man of confident and composed middle age, who went back to Benthamism once his youthful aberrations and early doubts were over. For these commentators, the epistemology of romanticism and the historical philosophy of French positivism were trivial and short-lived influences. Mill dallied with both, but there was no continuing relationship and no permanent consequences. This is considered very briefly in Chapter II, as part of the examination of Mill's utilitarianism, and further in Chapter V, as part of the problem of understanding the essay *On Liberty*. On the whole, however, the interpretation is unconvincing. Whatever regrets he had, Mill made no return to Benthamism worth speaking of: that kind of impetuous and argumentative rationalism was abandoned as a consequence of the crisis. The ambiguity in Mill's response to his education and instruction Mill himself never quite resolved, and his commentators cannot presume to do so either.

To some extent, I believe Mill's confidence in his own education was seriously misplaced and helped to perpetuate his difficulties. As one might expect, beginning again after six months of doubt and depression was neither simple nor straightforward, and Mill was much less well equipped than he imagined. As it turned out, the emphasis on the power of intellect, on the possession of rigorous and correctly made opinions, which was so appropriate for a Benthamite, was not very helpful in his own case. Given the right circumstances and the proper sequence of associations, the mind could indeed be made up in ordered and predictable ways. Opinions were relatively easy to alter, while new ideas could be quickly acquired. But changing habits, acquiring new sympathies and building up different dispositions, was far more difficult and far more demanding. The kind of passive sensationalism Mill had been taught by his father did not encourage the view that each person was capable of altering his own character, yet this was precisely what had to be done. Mill did not need new opinions; he needed a different character. The six months of crisis had forced him to take a close look at himself. He had worried and fretted, but this had not been so much about his ideas and opinions, as about his character and personal traits. He knew what he believed, but he constantly wondered what kind of person he was. This must be a demanding experience for any 20-year-old. For one as naïve as Mill, used to being told what to do by his father and then corrected for doing it wrongly, it was certain to be an awkward and profoundly disturbing experience. This is easily agreed, but Mill's concern to change his character and to alter his attitudes is perhaps less obvious. This may well explain why the theme of self-culture has not been given more attention by commentators. The source of the idea in English and German romanticism is also less well known than it might be. The notion, however, is surely crucial to Mill's conception of political theory, and Chapter I has an unwritten conclusion: that Mill's understanding of politics turned primarily upon a notion of self-culture or self-education derived from the English romantics and the German idealists; nowadays, when the point of reference is Coleridge at least, scholars are not greatly concerned to distinguish between the two.[5]

Neither this conclusion nor anything else in the book, however, establishes a definitive interpretation of Mill's political thinking, whether by reference to personal biography, or by repeated emphasis on a single significant theme like self-culture. This is not the result of ambiguities in Mill's thinking, nor of modesty or oversight in the author. It is the commonsense conclusion from a platitude, namely that there is no authoritative definition either of the subject matter or of the methods of political theory. There is, consequently, no formal or deliberate agreement to practise the activity in one way rather than another. Characteristically, political theorists work with loose and negotiable sets of concerns, making use of many different and varied skills. What works in one place may well fail in another, and success is precarious. In principle at least, the political theorist has a freedom of choice which is limited in only two general ways: first, by the contingencies of time, place and circumstance; secondly, by the restraints or limitations he chooses to impose upon himself. Each political theorist does what he can, with whatever ideas and skills are available to him. Interpreters are bound to do very much the same. They take only as much of Mill as they can presently use, selecting what they can explain and recommending what they can accept. Some aspects of a thinker are simply forgotten, others are neglected, and whatever the selection, the result is certain to be more than mere narrative, yet less than the original. For this reason, final or definitive interpretation is not an appropriate ambition. In the absence of common and formal criteria for determining what is correct and what is incorrect in the interpretation of ideas, it is difficult to see how things could be otherwise. All interpretation is selective, and all selection is arbitrary and partial. One can only hope the rationale of one's selection becomes convincing as the interpretation proceeds.

Notes (pp. 13–18)

1 The *Autobiography* was begun in the winter of 1853–4. Substantial revisions were made to this first draft in 1861 and again in 1869–70. There are now many examinations of the ambiguities of the *Autobiography*, as well as an increasing interest in the purely theoretical or speculative content of the work. Two examples of this interest are quite helpful: W. Thomas, 'John Stuart Mill and the Uses of Autobiography', *History*, vol. 56, no. 188, Oct. 1971, pp. 341–59; and R. D. Cumming, 'Mill's History of his Ideas', *Journal of the History of Ideas*, vol. xxv, no. 2, April–June 1964, pp. 235–56. On the writing, compilation and alterations between the various drafts of the *Autobiography*, see Jack Stillinger (ed.), *John Stuart Mill: Autobiography* (London, O.U.P., 1971), Introduction and notes; also, *The Early Draft of John Stuart Mill's Autobiography* (Urbana, Univ. of Illinois Press, 1961), and finally, 'The Text of John Stuart Mill's Autobiography', *Bulletin of the John Rylands Library*, vol. XLIII, 1960, pp. 220–42.

2 An amusing and perceptive account of Mill's life and personality can be found in Ruth Borchard, *John Stuart Mill: the Man* (London, Watts & Co., 1957). See in particular chs III–V dealing with Mill's conversion to Benthamism and his infatuation with Harriet Taylor. A less lively, more sombre and very respectful account is M. St J. Packe, *The Life of John Stuart Mill* (London, Secker & Warburg, 1954). Almost total adulation dominates W. L. Courtney, *The Life of John Stuart Mill* (London, Scott & Co., 1889).

3 Mill indulged in periodisation himself in an amateur way in the *Autobiography*, distinguishing three main periods in his 'mental progress' largely by reference to his major publications. Few commentators take this seriously, or bother to work out the implications of the division that Mill offers. There are two partial exceptions: J. M. Robson, *The Improvement of Mankind* (London, Routledge & Kegan Paul, 1968) and Alan Ryan, *J. S. Mill* (London, Routledge & Kegan Paul, 1974).

4 Mill to Carlyle, Oct. 1832, *The Earlier Letters of John Stuart Mill, 1812–1848* (Toronto, Univ. of Toronto Press, 1963), *Collected Works*, vol. XII, p. 128.

5 On the general question of Coleridge's indebtedness to German thinking, see G. N. G. Orsini, *Coleridge and German Idealism* (Carbondale, Southern Illinois Univ. Press, 1969). On the embarrassing and tricky problem of Coleridge's plagiarism of the German idealists, see Norman Fruman, *Coleridge, the Damaged Archangel* (London, George Allen & Unwin, 1972).

Chapter I

Self Culture,
the Eclectic Stance
and Toryism

In the autumn of 1826 and the winter of 1827, Mill had a nervous breakdown. Two aspects of that rather shapeless experience now seem significant. Mill was obviously overwhelmed by an enormous sense of personal inadequacy. He thought himself a complete failure, and worried about the cause of his doubts and depressions for six months, without ever finding a satisfactory answer. There was also a persistent feeling of guilt. Mill became more and more suspicious of his own responses. He was now inclined to blame himself for everything, fretting hopelessly about his own responsibility and treating every reaction as a sign of deep-seated deficiencies within himself. Also, while he was worrying about himself in this way, busily confirming the worst of his own fears and guiltily accepting the blame, he was also being nagged by the possible effects of his previous years of militancy. Several questions needed answering. Had four to five years of almost incessant sectarian controversy established irreversible traits? Were his dispositions now permanently fixed? Would his feelings always be like this? Whatever their naïvity, these were obvious questions to ask and the precise point of doubt was plain enough. Mill felt an urgent, almost desperate need to adopt a new character in order to prevent a deepening of his depression. But he doubted his own ability to do so. He saw himself as a hopeless case, facing a sudden and ignominious collapse. This is often ignored or slurred over by commentators; possibly out of sympathy, possibly out of embarrassment. Certainly it is easy to detect a kind of mawkish exaggeration common in many instances of adolescent heart searching, but since this was the most disturbing feature of the breakdown, condescension may be a little out of place. Mill had fallen apart. Although he was intellectually alive, he felt emotionally dead. He could think clearly enough, but there just seemed to be no point. Indeed, it was almost as if his father's austere and unnerving prediction had already come true. He was now 'unfit for all the common purposes of life'. Two lines of Coleridge conveyed this sense of dissociated experience and were quoted in the *Autobiography*.

Work without hope draws nectar in a sieve,
And hope without an object cannot live.[1]

Mill was nothing if not conscientious, however. He could never live with doubts, even when those doubts were about himself; his old habits simply would not let him. With that kind of massive dedication and intense seriousness which led Carlyle to label the *Autobiography* the life of a steam engine, Mill began to probe the exact nature of his limitations. He read through the whole of Byron's published works, for instance, 'to try whether a poet, whose peculiar department was supposed to be that of the intenser feelings, could rouse any feeling in me'. This had no appreciable effect: 'The poet's state of mind was too like my own.'[2] Mill now feared the worst. Very nervously, he imagined even more serious weaknesses within himself, and at every moment during these months of depression obviously expected to find the final and decisive flaw. This was nerve racking; doubt piled on doubt, giving Mill an even deeper sense of despair about himself. The first substantial relief came only by accident while reading Marmontel's *Memoirs*. Mill discovered he was still capable of generous feelings, he could respond as a complete human being. 'I was no longer hopeless: I was not a stock or a stone. I had still, it seemed, some of the material out of which all worth of character, and all capacity for happiness, are made.'[3] He felt alive again.

In Mill's case, accidental relief also led to firm conviction: the change and development of his own character was a necessary condition for any future progress. Although doubts and depressions returned again briefly in the summer of 1828 and more seriously on the death of his father, Mill was now sustained by a conviction that with proper attention to his own make up, there would be no return of the depression he had just experienced. Mill's mood could hardly be described as buoyant. He was hopeful rather than confident, but this was a crucial moment all the same. Mill now had an unavoidable commitment to self-culture: a commitment sustained by deep personal anxiety about the future and by feelings of guilt about the past. He desperately needed to believe that each person determined his own character and was capable of bringing about changes if he so desired. His own future appeared to rest on the truth of this proposition. Almost inevitably, this wholly new emphasis on the constitutive power of the will brought Mill face to face with the psychological orthodoxies of Benthamism. In some of its forms

at least, the doctrine of associationism had made each individual the
the derivative product of previous instruction and experience. The
individual was fixed by common circumstance and set in his ways by
unalterable sensations. Mill's own depression, in fact, had been deep-
ened by this very idea. He had thought his character fixed at the time of
the crisis, taking his sufferings to be 'the natural effect of causes that it
was hardly possible for time to remove'.⁴ After all, he had always been
taught that the individual was not directly responsible for his own
character. This was made for him and not by him, and while the dogmas
of associationism might encourage a form of moral utopianism, where
everything was possible once circumstances were altered, they also
encouraged a kind of personal fatalism. Everyone should resign himself
to his character as it was. This was the first point of serious confronta-
tion with Benthamism.

As is well known, the Benthamite orthodoxy was mechanical materialism or passive sensationalism. The label is relatively unimportant. The
first is more familiar to political theorists, the second to psychologists;
but both are adequate. While 'mechanical' conveys the dominant
analogy of the artefact or machine, 'passive' points to the quiet and
quiescent role accorded to the mind. We should remember the images of
Locke; images emphasising the initial passivity of the mind as well as
its physical construction. The mind was an empty cabinet, a dark room
and a blank sheet. Following Locke, Hobbes, Hartley and Priestley,
the Benthamites took all elements in the mind's make up to be derivative and secondary consequences of phenomena in nature. This is a
gross simplification, of course, but knowledge was held to pose no
special problem for natural science. Knowledge was a particular
combination of sensation and perception: a combination set up in the
mind as a result of external stimuli. There was no problem either about
reflection. Reflection was nothing but consciousness; consciousness, in
turn, was nothing but sensation, and sensation was response to stimuli.
To reflect on an idea, therefore, was identical with having an idea,
ideas themselves, according to the Benthamites, being only a class or
combination of sensation or feeling, 'which exists after the object of
sense has ceased to be present'.⁵ In short, the mind was acted upon,
passively receiving and making up impressions from outside. Impulse,
feeling, meditation, even the complexities of sensibility, all were explicable by the same principle. Consequently, the mind itself, as Coleridge
had seen in his study of Kant, could so easily be reduced to a mere
assembly of mechanical movements whose workings were best explained
by analogy to the 'Aeolian Harp' played by the wind, or to 'a barrel
organ turned by a stream of water'.⁶ Whatever analogy was used, the
mind was strictly determined by the phenomena of nature.

This determinist conception of the mind generated a distinct philosophy of education. Given an understanding of the laws governing the make up of the mind, an understanding which could be just as exact as in mechanics, a succession of sensations and an association of ideas could be produced which would infallibly lead to correct conduct. A teacher could inculcate whatever values he chose, simply by associating these values with the sensations of pleasure. There were only two limitations of any consequence. One was imposed by simple ignorance of the universal laws of association, the other stemmed from the inadequacy of the means available for instructing the mind. These were severe but far from conclusive limits. Just as the mind received sensations which then combined in a regular and definite manner, so it could also receive particular sets of pleasurable and painful associations which would ultimately provoke correct action. The mind could become an assembly of wants and aversions producing the correct associations in a fixed sequence over and over again, time after time. As James Mill so patiently explained: 'as all the actions of man are produced by his feelings or thoughts, the business of education is, to make certain feelings or thoughts take place instead of others. The business of education, then, is to work upon the mental successions'.[7] Not surprisingly perhaps, James Mill strongly approved of Helvetius's famous comment '*l'éducation peut tout*'.

Mill knew this orthodoxy very well of course. He had grown up with the phenomenal and experiential philosophy. His instruction was that ideas were regulative only; and we might also remember that the reduction of mental phenomena to banks of sensation associated by laws of resemblance and contiguity was high philosophic fashion in his youth. The Utilitarian Society itself had chosen Hartley as a canonical text. The members, including Mill, assembled specifically to study Priestley's edition. Indeed, they had forced up the price of the book 'by searching through London to furnish each of us with a copy'.[8] They had also reassembled to continue discussion of analytic psychology when James Mill's *Analysis of the Phenomena of the Human Mind* was first published. As a part of his domestic routine, Mill had also 'read the manuscript, portion by portion, as it advanced'.[9] There was no problem, then, about familiarity. Associationism was a part of Mill's life; he knew it by heart, and no doubt he formed views about many issues through these and related studies. 'Hartleian metaphysics' led in many directions, not just one. Certainly, the questions raised by Hartley were never thought to be solely or narrowly epistemological, and his father's mode of analysing mental phenomena was capable of extension to other phenomena. To Mill himself, associationism was the crucial theory which enabled special and complex mental phenomena to be reduced to more general and more simple phenomena, covered by a small number of

23

laws. In effect, the theory of association of ideas made the Newtonian approach feasible. Mill never doubted that and he was always quick to defend Hartley and Priestley against all attacks. Immediately after the breakdown, however, Mill was mainly concerned with one implication. If associationism and sensationalism were true, then each person's character and conduct was ready made for him: the individual thought and acted as past experience and previous instruction necessitated. Unless external circumstances altered, altering in turn the source, nature and combination of sensations, then character and conduct was permanently fixed. No wonder Mill was depressed. He seemed compelled to be a helpless spectator to his own misfortune. The individual was trapped by circumstance: a passive and manufactured object not an active, responsible agent. He explained the effect of this doctrine in the *Autobiography*. 'Philosophical Necessity', as Mill labelled it, 'weighed on my existence like an incubus. I felt as if I was scientifically proved to be the helpless slave of antecedent circumstances; as if my character and that of all others had been formed for us by agencies beyond our control, and was wholly out of our own power.'[10]

There is no ambiguity here; and 'incubus' was an appropriate word to use, capturing the mood of the moment quite well. Mill was indeed haunted by a persistent sense of hopelessness. As it stood, associationism was a doctrine of despair edging Mill into a state of futility. After his experience of doubt and depression, much of it guiltily blamed upon himself, Mill needed confirmation of the ability to control and to change personal character. The orthodoxies he had been taught gave precisely the opposite assurance. If the organisation and relationship of the faculties was permanently fixed, then there could be no future for Mill different from the present. His own education had already let him down very badly. His ideological commitments had not prevented complete misery, and his militant activities as a Benthamite were now a serious embarrassment. Looking back, there had been far too much sectarian controversy; far too much dogmatic analysis and not enough generous sympathy. This sense of hopelessness, combined with acute embarrassment at the past, gave Mill a very clear view of what was required. In order to demonstrate a control over character and to express a dislike of the past, Mill felt that he had to avoid any kind of sectarian controversy. It was almost as if the power of each individual to be what he chose to be could be demonstrated only by acquiring a calm and considered detachment. The reason is clear and we will not dwell on it. The ethos of the Benthamite school had always been set by the profession of strong opinion, by a single-minded dedication to the removal of abuse and error and by an earnest and argumentative enthusiasm. Mill now deliberately chose the opposite or contrasting qualities.

Self-culture would proceed by demonstrating a capacity for generous feelings. Mill would now quietly cultivate sympathetic and disinterested concerns. He would certainly avoid entanglement in narrow causes. He would, in short, set out to become an eclectic. This was a decision with permanent consequences for Mill's political thinking, and even if we cannot date the decision very precisely, we can quite easily recognise the disposition. The choice of an open and eclectic stance was meant as a refutation. If Mill could become other than a narrow and manufactured radical, then his education and instruction would have had a conclusion different to the one intended and predicted. Mill would then be able to believe fully in 'what is really inspiriting and ennobling in the doctrine of free will', that 'we have real power over the formation of our own character'.[11] In effect, the logic of fatalism was to be refuted by the practice of self-culture.

To begin with, then, Mill's eclecticism was mainly a condemnation of his past, far stronger in self-denial than in anything else. He had no time for sectarianism, he had no heart for militancy. All headstrong commitment to single principles and to sole truths starved the faculties, and dogmatism made a full meal of experience impossible. Mill took this to be the main lesson of his own past. Quite deliberately, he turned his back on his training for activism. 'I had now learnt by experience that the passive susceptibilities needed to be cultivated as well as the active capacities.'[12] He was also in a position now to be convinced of the dull and unimaginative ethos of utilitarian rationalism. His former teachers and colleagues had so obviously neglected the varieties of individual experience. They had been far too concerned with universal methods and with a blank, analytic rigour. Mill could no longer support this. If it was not false or misconceived in principle, the effect was still to encourage a dogmatic and sententious spirit. In effect, Mill had chosen an attitude of mind rather than a policy, a disposition rather than a new theory. He would have no single system of ideas. He would not be exclusive in his opinions. He would, instead, seek to hold a kind of balance where analysis was matched by feeling, science by poetry and action by contemplation. While suspending belief in one grand and comprehensive theory, he would judge all systems and all ideas instrumentally, constantly assessing their capacity to diffuse sympathy, tolerance and imagination more widely. These were the qualities crucial to eclecticism. They prevented the mind from carrying out a uniform, humdrum and merely passive set of operations. They were proof that the relationship of the faculties was not fixed by wholly private and internal combinations of pain and pleasure. All of these responses might have been expected. Mill was acutely embarrassed by his own past. More and more, however, he was constrained by a concern

Coláiste Oideachais Máire Gan Smal Luimneach 30,055

to avoid controversy and dispute and although he was free to look anywhere for true eclectic qualities, he began to look in particular at those ideas capable of inspiring broad agreement. His eclecticism became increasingly bland and apologetic, and this helps to explain the attraction of the French Saint-Simonian thinkers, about which commentators constantly disagree.[13]

No matter the particular doctrines they advocated, about industrial production, about the role of women or about the alternation of organic and critical periods in history, Mill was most strongly impressed by the Saint-Simonian reaction against the militant *école critique* of the previous century. He always treated the Saint-Simonians as examples of a new age of agreement. Whatever their faults, they were the honest forerunners of an increasing tendency towards sympathetic association in European society. They possessed the very opposite qualities to the radicals he had previously worked with. 'Generous enthusiasm' was a phrase he often used and it is clear what he meant. The Saint-Simonians offered a broad and humane social idea, not a narrow, political creed. They placed the emphasis on sacrifice rather than satisfaction and on conscience rather than interest. Their specific aim, of course, was to replace egoism by altruism, so bringing the brotherhood of man closer. They also had a philosophy of history which led them to accept the validity of many different kinds of historical experience. They seemed at first glance at least, to have avoided the inhibiting rationalist assumption of a uniform human nature: an assumption which had led so often to an extreme parochialism and to a disdain for other than European cultures. All of their beliefs, in fact, pointed with modest confidence to an increased agreement among all kinds and classes of people. And from the time that Gustave d'Eichthal attended the London Debating Society in May 1828 as one of the two Saint-Simonian missionaries to England, until the break up of the school after its suppression and trial in Paris in 1832, Mill invariably praised them for offering a live example of eclecticism. Their whole ethos was appealing. They had a spirit of 'comprehensive liberality': 'a spirit opposed to the spirit of criticism and disceptation'; a spirit concerned to appropriate 'that portion or fragment (however diminutive) of truth, which there must necessarily be at the bottom of every error'.[14] This was the aspect of Saint-Simonianism which had given the French the initiative in political theory: not, Mill explained, 'from the number of truths which have yet been practically arrived at, but rather from the more elevated *terrain* on which the discussion is engaged'.[15]

Mill was very well aware, however, of the sectarian tendencies of the Saint-Simonians themselves. They could hardly be missed. And although Mill got on exceptionally well with the first Saint-Simonian missionaries to England, he soon noticed a persistent desire to adopt the trappings of a dogmatic faith and to follow the procedures of a hierarchical church. Enfantin even retired to a monastery, gathering together a coterie of the faithful and proclaiming himself the new St John. Comte also troubled Mill. He was far too fanatical and far too single-minded to be a true eclectic. There was altogether too much enthusiasm. Comte obviously lacked the bland and patient benevolence which promoted the exercise of eclectic imagination. Like most French philosophers in Mill's view, he would insist 'upon only seeing one thing when there are many, or seeing a thing only on one side, only in one point of view when there are many others equally essential to a just estimate of it'.[16] Indeed, Mill was neither swamped by Saint-Simonian ideas, nor completely convinced by the first emissaries to England. His correspondence with d'Eichthal is a fine example of how he agreed just enough to be able to exchange ideas, but never quite enough to be thought a disciple. Presumably, this was the correct attitude. The eclectic should never be fully committed to a single theory, yet he had to be sufficiently engaged in order to understand that theory. He could have knowledge, but never blind faith. Even so, despite his reservations, Mill was strongly attracted. The Saint-Simonian view of truth and falsity, which rested upon a sensitive historical relativism, was particularly appealing. More and more, Mill was inclined to relate political theory to a positive philosophy of history which took political knowledge to be contingent upon knowledge of the future. He acknowledged this quite bluntly in a letter to d'Eichthal. The Saint-Simonians were the first to point out that 'the first step in the investigation of practical political truths' was 'to ascertain what is the state into which, in the natural order of the advancement of civilisation the nation in question will next come; in order that it may be the grand object of our endeavours, to facilitate the transition to this state'.[17] In Mill's view, politics was a progressive science just because it considered 'views which ascend high into the past, and stretch far into the future'.[18]

There was, of course, no shortage of other ideas to be examined, and the Saint-Simonian thinkers were not the only influences. Mill had the intellectual capacity, the classical education and a sufficient smattering of foreign languages to borrow from many and varied sources. In itself, this presented no problem. Mill read German theology, Greek tragedy, medieval science and contemporary poetry with equal relish. Obviously, the eclectic should read widely. He should acquire knowledge wherever it could be found, putting together as many partial truths as possible. But, even so, doubts remained, and Mill wondered whether he would be able to sustain sufficient excitement and enough freshness to appreciate ideas properly. One can see the point of doubt.

The true quality of the eclectic mind was not acquisition as such. It was more like an ability to grasp ideas and opinions, not only different from one's own, but also alien in spirit and conception. The demand was not for analytic capacity, but for the exercise of a strong and sympathetic imagination. One had to feel what others had felt, sharing in their experience rather than simply copying it. Mill was very slow indeed to realise his capacity for this kind of experience. This was part of the naïvity we have already mentioned, but it was also a legacy of his education. He had never been taught that the feelings could be educated and developed as well as the mind. Wordsworth was the decisive influence here, and we have to examine this influence in some detail.

Mill read a good deal of Wordsworth during the autumn of 1828, and in January of the following year he defended him at the London Debating Society in reply to Roebuck's championing of Byron. The speech lasted two and three-quarter hours. It was the first public confession of Mill's new way of thinking. In it, he referred to all of Wordsworth's major poems including 'Intimations of Immortality', 'Tintern Abbey' and 'The Solitary Reaper'. Only the notes for the speech survive,[19] but these are enough to establish what Mill thought he had learnt from Wordsworth. Mill informed his audience that he now saw poetry as 'an important branch of education. Education is 1. the education of the intellect; 2. that of the feelings. Folly of supposing that the first suffices without the last'. The tone is not one of disenchantment; there is no quality of sad or wistful resignation. Mill spoke convinced and confident of his ability to become a true eclectic, and he was clear what this involved. 'There is no depth, no intensity, no force, in our descriptions of feelings unless we have ourselves experienced the feelings we describe.' Mill was also certain that he owed it all to Wordsworth.

> I have learned from Wordsworth that it is possible by dwelling on certain ideas [and by] a proper regulation of the associations to keep up a constant freshness in the emotions which objects excite and which else they would cease to excite as we grow older—to connect cheerful and joyous states of mind with almost every object, to make everything speak to us of our own enjoyments or those of other sentient beings, and to multiply ourselves as it were in the enjoyments of other creatures: to make the good parts of human nature afford us more pleasure than the bad parts afford us pain—and to rid ourselves entirely of all feelings of hatred or scorn for our fellow creatures.

These are the words of someone who had turned right away from mechanical materialism and passive sensationalism towards the common standpoint implied by emotional experience. Two years after the speech, in 1831, Mill visited Wordsworth during a four-week walking tour of the Lake District.[20] On his return to London, the conversion had been completed. Mill now held Wordsworth to be the perfect embodiment of eclecticism. The 'extensive range of his thoughts and the largeness and expansiveness of his feelings', the 'extreme comprehensiveness and philosophic spirit which is in him', made him 'the direct antithesis of what the Germans most expressively call onesidedness'. In this, Mill added, he was very different from 'radicals and utilitarians': generally, they see 'only one side of the subject'.[21]

All of these remarks, about Comte, about Wordsworth and about the Saint-Simonians, point in the same direction. Within two or three years of the crisis, the pursuit of eclecticism had turned Mill against militancy and against controversy. The politics of active public commitment were now over. Mill had turned his back on the past, showing this most of all by a growing reluctance to confront and to examine differences between ideas. More and more, he inclined to the view that it was not the job of an eclectic to refute anything. This was an ugly and hectoring business, and all ideas contained some truth. Mill became studiously pliant and massively sympathetic, listening to all ideas and opinions, tolerating every point of view, endeavouring to see good in them all. He admitted to Carlyle that he had become 'catholic and tolerant in an extreme degree' at this time, scarcely feeling himself 'called upon to *deny* anything but Denial itself'.[22] Partly, no doubt, this was a belated retraction of his early aggressive habits; a form of apology for previous errors. But Mill's response to his own radical past was also the beginning of a settled conception of political argument. As an eclectic, Mill now held all argument *a priori*, no matter how rigorous, to be completely inappropriate. First principles and universal axioms were an encumbrance. They made persuasion difficult; they tended to promote irreconcilable controversies. What mattered, in any case, were not final reasons or justifications and the deductions which could be made to follow from them, but the common sympathies arising from shared experiences. The political philosopher should be less concerned with the delineation of principle than with understanding the circumstances in which agreement was possible. And the commonsense conclusion was that he should always draw attention to secondary and intermediate maxims, Baconian *vera illa et media axiomata*, upon which all people could proceed to reach pragmatic compromises. This view of political philosophy had many implications. Refutation became insignificant and explanation was replaced by understanding. There was also a certain relativism involved, but one implication was particularly significant: consensus became the main or prime value and Mill began to preach the politics of agreement.

In May 1832, for instance, Mill reviewed Cornewall Lewis's *Use and*

Abuse of Political Terms.[23] The review was broadly favourable and later on Mill was to write that it painted 'exactly the state of my mind and feelings at that time'.[24] The review gave full expression to Mill's eclecticism and to his dislike of discursive reasoning about principle. The proper office of a clear thinker was not analysis at all, he argued, but sympathetic exposition. The true thinker avoided controversy, preferring instead to make 'other men's thoughts clear for them'. 'A man must now learn', Mill continued, 'to look upon all things with a benevolent, but upon great men and their works with a reverential spirit.' There was certainly no lack of confidence. Consensus would be reached. The 'great philosophical achievement of the era' was close at hand. Soon it would be possible 'to unite all half-truths, which have been fighting against one another ever since the creation, and blend them in one harmonious whole'. This same cheerful optimism showed itself elsewhere. While reviewing Blakey's *History of Moral Science*, a book he thoroughly disapproved of, Mill still found room for delighted surprise at just how few questions of 'practical morals, require for their determination any premisses but such as are common to all philosophic sects'.[25] In Mill's case, the first blush of eclecticism had prompted optimism as well as pragmatism. The appeal to secondary or intermediate maxims could be unrestrained and confident because of the strong probability that such maxims would be commonly accepted. Only sectarians would continue to argue about principles in politics.

This full-scale retreat from dispute and from criticism was the dominant theme in Mill's thinking in the years immediately after the crisis, but it was by no means confined to his published writings. He also began to live the life of an impartial and benevolent eclectic. He left the London Debating Society in 1829. 'I object to placing myself in the situation of an advocate for or against a cause,' he informed d'Eichthal, adding that he objected to controversy precisely because it kept up the *esprit critique*.[26] Looking back on the event in the *Autobiography*, he made no bones about his reasons. 'I had had enough of speech-making, and was glad to carry on my private studies and meditations without any immediate call for outward assertion of their results.'[27] Consequently Mill wrote very little at this time and nothing regularly for publication. He did publish a long and critical review of Sir Walter Scott's *Life of Buonaparte* in the *Westminster Review* for April 1828, and he found room to damn 'narrow and partial observation' and to praise 'enlarged experience'.[28] Also, in the two years between 1829 and 1831, he furthered his knowledge of Greek literature and civilisation. He translated and annotated several of Plato's dialogues, four of these annotated translations, the *Protagoras*, the *Gorgias*, the *Phaedrus* and the *Apology*, being published in the *Monthly Repository*. Indeed, the eclectic ideal and the Greek experience were very close. Plato had been instrumental in Mill's recovery from the breakdown, and Socrates' notion of his vocation in the *Phaedrus*, as a kind of mental midwife delivering the truth of many ideas, was strictly analogous to the role Mill had adopted for himself. He was bound to assist the birth of truth whenever and wherever he could, but truth would neither be conceived nor quickened in conditions of conflict, nor would it be arrived at by means of narrow commitment. For this reason, Mill was very careful to steer clear of popular and acrimonious disputes. This was so, for instance, with the agitation for the first Reform Bill. He did give some token support here and there; he attended the occasional meeting, made small financial contributions to the Parliamentary Candidates Society and to the National Political Union, but the gestures were without enthusiasm. Mill had no heart for controversy, and after the Lords had rejected the Bill on the second reading in October 1831, he confessed to John Sterling just how little he cared for public political agitation, adding that 'the time is not yet come when a calm and impartial person can intermeddle with advantage'.[29]

Nothing could be much clearer than this, and it enables us to pull the threads together without too much trouble. The choice of an eclectic stance had been originally taken as a confirmation of free will. A person's ability to change his character if he so desired was sufficient refutation of the fatalism implied by the doctrine of 'Philosophic Necessity'. In Mill's case, the commitment to self-culture was taken at a time of acute embarrassment with the past. Consequently, the eclectic stance increasingly entailed a retreat from militancy and a withdrawal from active public life. This was not out of lethargy or out of apathy, not at least in any ordinary sense of these words. As Mill understood them, the activities of self-culture were synonymous with a constant and strenuous self-improvement. Self-culture was hard work and Mill was firmly committed, of course, to acquiring all of the characteristics of tolerance and to establishing firm habits of benevolence as quickly as possible. He had not adopted a theory or a philosophy, so much as an attitude of mind. The question of criteria, then, is particularly difficult: how was self-culture to be assessed? One simple test was the extent to which sympathy had grown. Sympathy was the essential eclectic quality. Without it, there could be no sharing of diverse experiences and none of the agreements arising from common responses. A plain lack of concern was fatal in all respects. Obviously, self-culture was bound to rule out indifference, but if indifference was ruled out, so was the adoption of any one set of opinions. The eclectic was not concerned with opinions as such anyway. He was concerned with feelings and dispositions and with the elevation and refinement of

31

the affections; 'fitting him to look abroad and see how he is to act, not imposing upon him by express definition, a prescribed mode of action'.[30] The eclectic was also the free spirit.

The echo of Wordsworth in all of this is very clear. Sympathetic interest in the common feelings and common destiny of human beings was a mark of true education. Like Wordsworth, Mill believed this could only take place once the 'inward passions' and not 'outward arrangements' had been cultivated. But there are other echoes as well: Macaulay's criticism of utilitarianism had also played a part. Mill very much appreciated his rejection of abstract, *a priori* reasoning in politics and he was also convinced by Macaulay's contention that human motives were never final and fixed. He did find the bantering tone of Macaulay's writings somewhat regrettable; they were too polemical and too dismissive. At the same time, however, his father's reaction to these writings had provided ample confirmation of the intolerant and narrow ethos which underpinned the Benthamite system. James Mill simply treated Macaulay's arguments as irrational, dismissing them as 'an attack upon the reasoning faculty'. 'This made me think that there was really something more fundamentally erroneous in my father's conception of philosophical Method, as applicable to politics, than I had hitherto supposed there was.'[31]

At times, perhaps, there was more than a little adolescent heart searching in Mill's pursuit of eclecticism. Occasionally, his attempts at aesthetic education may only have resulted in rather morbid doubts about intention and motive. But his own self-culture had a persistent logic which it would be foolish to ignore. If he of all people could overcome the narrow and disputatious character of a militant, then others could certainly do so. The covert assumption of self-culture was common agreement. No one was sectarian by nature; no one made dogmatic by instruction need remain so. If people abandoned belief in first principles and single truths applicable to all times and places, there would be greater scope for compromise and for accommodation. So, although the very inwardness of self-culture was appealing to Mill, there was a general or public conclusion to be drawn. Like the eclectic, everyone could learn to match truth and falsity to historical circumstance: like the eclectic, they ought to be convinced that in politics now one theory was right, now another. Looking back on these years, the years of the late twenties and early thirties, it is hardly surprising that Mill wrote of his '*sortie définitive de la section benthamiste de l'école révolutionnaire*'.[32] He had indeed quit the radical camp. The eclectic principle had issued in a quiet and confident pragmatism. Mill sought moderation issue by issue, and he was now happiest when contemplating the virtues of agreement. He had even raised the issue of his own quietism during the debating speech on Wordsworth. Was it the case, he asked, that Wordsworth's morality tended to make men quietists, 'to make them bear'? Undoubtedly it was. But,

'allow that a habit of bearing those evils, which can be avoided, is a bad habit. But because there are some things which ought not to be borne, does it follow that there is no use even now, in learning to bear many evils even now which must be borne: hope the time will come when no evils but those arising from the necessary constitution of man and of external nature'.[33]

The extent of Mill's contentment can be gauged by his next comment. He told his audience 'how much more there is to aim at when we see that happiness may coexist with being stationary and does not require us to keep moving'.

For several years after the crisis, then, certainly from 1829 until the beginnings of Mill's attempt to reorganise the radical party in the middle of the thirties, the pursuit of eclecticism had been matched by the development of an ideal and contemplative toryism. This is a poor label. While 'ideal' serves its purpose, 'tory' is not quite to the point since there was no great pessimism about human nature and no attachment to prejudice as such. 'Contemplative' may also obscure the strong commitment to proselytise secondary maxims and to promote agreement at every opportunity. But the label fits where it touches. Mill had become a determined opponent of sectarian radicalism in these years. He now disliked militancy, preferring to restrain and to reconcile. He carefully shunned all narrow-minded commitment. He found the philosophy of manufacturing distasteful, taking it to be a confirmation of the sordid narrowness of the age. He also obviously enjoyed contemplating the virtues of agreement; 'there never was, and never will be, a virtuous people where there is not unanimity, or an agreement nearly approaching to it, in their notions of virtue'.[34] Appropriately enough, he had also begun to oppose arguments for the sovereignty of the individual. The passions of the turbulent individual needed to be quietly restrained, and like all good tories, Mill was very worried by exercises of the popular will. The sovereignty of the people was a delegated sovereignty, to be exercised through familiar representatives, not a sovereignty which implied the unsteady practice of referring public questions to the suffrages of the people. In the summer of 1832, in two articles in the *Examiner*, Mill criticised radical theories of representation, particularly the doctrine of pledges. He asserted 'that the test of what is right in politics is not the *will* of the people, but the *good* of the people, and our object is, not to compel but to persuade the people to impose, for the sake of their own good, some restraint on the immediate and unlimited exercise of their own will'.[35] And while we may worry about the appropriateness of our label, many of Mill's contemporaries were absolutely convinced. These two articles alone lost the *Examiner* many radical readers because of their tory sentiments.

There was also an abundance of tory style and sentiment in Mill's ascetic disdain for the dull and businesslike manner of the English. The English, unfortunately, were vulgar and insensitive materialists. As a nation they were inferior to the French. They also lagged well behind the Prussians who had devised local and municipal institutions for the free expression of national spirit. Like the British government in India, the Prussians were not afraid of the aristocratic principle. They saw the importance of special expertise in government and in the conduct of public affairs. Their government was 'a most powerfully and skilfully organised aristocracy of all the most highly educated men in the kingdom'. Political questions were not decided 'by an appeal, either direct or indirect, to the judgement or will of an uninstructed mass, whether of gentlemen or of clowns; but by the de-liberately-formed opinions of a comparatively few, specially educated for the task'.[36] The *Autobiography* gave full expression to these grouses about the English. Mill lamented the condition of the ordinary English who lacked an 'interest in things of an unselfish kind, except occasion-ally in a special thing here and there'. Their feelings and intellectual qualities remained undeveloped, 'reducing them, considered as spiritual beings, to a kind of negative existence'.[37] Consequently, while Mill's toryism was not attached by custom or prejudice to privileged institutions of church and state, or to the immemorial prerogatives of the owning classes, there was nevertheless a reverence for government animated by ideals and recruited from among the specially educated. This was one way to improve national character. And in an age dominated by a relent-less materialism, strong and expert government was essential for the good of the people. So although Mill's toryism tended to be quiet and contemplative rather than loud and strident, there was no room for indifference or for apathy. Everyone should endeavour to improve himself, always keeping busy with the activities of self-culture. Only in this way would the individual act as an example to others, so helping to improve and to elevate the national character. Without these activities, the English would remain dead and dispirited, their politics would con-tinue to be a shadow of their materialism and the work of individual culture would either be left undone, or organised for the purposes of political control by one narrow sect or party. Our label does indeed seem justified: as Mill became an eclectic, so he also became a tory.

These high-minded tory themes appear again and again in the writings of the late twenties and early thirties. They dominate Mill's contributions to the dissenting *Monthly Repository*, under the editorship of William Johnson Fox. They are also prominent in his articles and reviews for the weekly magazine the *Examiner*, edited by Albany Fonblanque, and in his contributions to *Tait's Edinburgh Magazine*. The letters, particularly those to Sterling and Carlyle, regularly present an ideal and contemplative toryism. It is surprising how little attention these writings have received: only one of them is regularly referred to, that which was published in the *Examiner* between January and May 1831, entitled 'The Spirit of the Age', and even this is often used simply to show an indebtedness to the Saint-Simonians.[38] This series of articles, however, contained many emphases. There was the eclectic stress on agreement: 'the first men of the age will one day join hands and be agreed; and then there is no power in itself, on earth or in hell, capable of withstanding them'. There was also an emphasis on free inquiry appropriate to an ethic of self-culture: 'everyone must judge for himself as he best may'. But the overwhelming stress falls on the aristocratic principle, on the need for an ascendancy 'of the most virtuous and best instructed of the nation'. The third of the five articles made this absolutely clear. 'Society may be said to be in its natural state, when worldly power, and moral influence, are habitually and undisputably exercised by the fittest persons whom the existing state of Society affords.'[39] The disposition is manifestly tory, whether or not the Saint-Simonians were the immediate influence.

Mill took the opportunity to develop all of these themes further in the form of an anonymous commentary on the philosophy of Bentham. Anonymity was no luxury since Mill was still living at his father's house in Kensington; he was also his subordinate at work in India House. The anonymous commentary was bitter and hostile. Bentham was completely ignorant of human nature; his system was narrow, mean and selfish; his writings did more harm than good. As a tory, Mill was also sure precisely where Benthamism had failed. While it might be adequate as a philosophy of legislation, it 'will be most apt to fail in the consideration of the greater social questions—the theory of organic institutions and general forms of polity; for those (unlike the details of legislation) to be duly estimated, must be viewed as the great instruments of forming the national character; of carrying forward the members of the community towards perfection, or preserving them from degeneracy'.[40] The aristocratic principle was necessary to improve national character.

We should not minimise the ideal character of this toryism, however. Mill himself made a distinction between toryism as it usually was and toryism as it might be or was only exceptionally. He considered himself an ideal tory, above sectarian creed, beyond sectional interest and distant from the littleness of politics. He wrote a long letter to John Sterling in October 1831, for instance, starkly contrasting 'practical' with 'ideal' toryism: practical toryism was narrow, mean and unimaginative, being little more than the selfishness of 'the place-hunter and jobber'; as a creed, it was totally incompatible 'with any large and generous aspirations', often meaning 'being *in*, and availing yourself of your comfortable position *inside* the vehicle without minding the poor devils who are freezing outside'. Practical toryism, in fact, was the smug and self-centred philosophy of the establishment. Ideal toryism, on the other hand, the toryism of such as Wordsworth and Coleridge, was wholly admirable. These tories showed a proper reverence for government and for a fair distribution of its benefits. They were also 'duly sensible that it is good for man to be ruled; to submit both his body and mind to the guidance of a higher intelligence and virtue. It is therefore the direct antithesis of liberalism, which is for making every man his own guide and sovereign master, and letting him think for himself and do exactly as he judges best for himself'. Mill left Sterling in no doubt where he stood. Liberalism, in Mill's view, showed a 'thorough ignorance of man's nature, and of what is necessary for his happiness or what degree of happiness and virtue he is capable of attaining'.[41]

This reverence for government and for noble and inspired leadership attracted Mill to Coleridge's idea of a nationally endowed clergy or clerisy. He had read the essay *On the Constitution of the Church and State* a little over a year after it had been published. There were two copies of the essay in his library. He also quoted extensively from it in 1833 in his own essay on 'Corporation and Church Property'. Coleridge's presentation of the spiritual mission of the clergy obviously made a deep impression. This has puzzled most commentators. Some cannot imagine how a religious sceptic, brought up to show contempt for 'extra-experimental belief' and for the 'sacerdotal class', could possibly welcome an endowed clergy. Others are absolutely certain that it shows Mill to be a subtle and devious authoritarian, welcoming any device to promote consensus.[42] Neither of these responses is appropriate. Mill's view was very simple. A non-sectarian learned class would help to protect the nation against mediocrity and indifference, the two main threats to self-culture. The clerisy would teach others by their own example, acting as any national church ought to act, as a vehicle of spiritual improvement. They would not all teach the same thing, however, nor would they teach different things in the same way. The clerisy would be both non-doctrinal and non-dogmatic, the paradigm being any body of well-educated and tolerant eclectics. The mistake, as Mill explained to James Martineau,

36

'is in applying the *test* to the *doctrines* which the clergy shall teach, instead of applying it to their qualifications as teachers, and to the spirit in which they teach. When you give a man a diploma as a physician, you do not bind him to follow a prescribed method; you merely assure yourself of his being duly *acquainted* with what is known or believed on the subject, and of his having competent powers of mind. I would do the same with clergymen'.[43]

For this reason, there could be no question of sectarian recruitment. Anyone who was 'capable of producing a beneficial effect on their age and country as teachers of the knowledge which fits people to perform their duties and exercise their rights' could be included in the clerisy. Even non-christians might be considered. 'No church not founded on this comprehensive principle, can, or ought to stand.'[44] Mill maintained this consistently. Everything depended on spirit and attitude. The clerisy was like a school. While it did not suppose its teachers to be in possession of absolute truth, neither did it take its pupils to be fixed in ignorance. Each could learn from the other, but only if the other was learned and inspired enough to be a good teacher. If there was agreement, it would derive from conviction and persuasion.

When all of these many articles, reviews and letters are taken together, it is possible to put the nature of Mill's toryism beyond reasonable doubt. It was the politics of poetry: a quest for inspiration and for imagination in a prosaic world; a search for leadership and for guidance above the littleness of the age. Indeed, the analogy to poetry is instructive. Like poetry, Mill's toryism was many-sided in its pursuit of experience: like poetry, it offered a permanent criticism of the ordinary, the commonplace and the merely mundane. As a more specific attitude, a middle way was sought between the sectarian enthusiasms of the rationalists, on the one hand, and the servility of those who were merely time serving on the other. The overall tone was a quiet and considered idealism, stressing conscience rather than expediency, virtue rather than interest and putting sacrifice before satisfaction. Above all, perhaps, the ideal tory should be concerned with national character. He should promote those elevated social feelings essential to a common nationality: not nationality 'in the vulgar sense of the term; a senseless antipathy to foreigners; an indifference to the general welfare of the human race'. 'We mean a principle of sympathy, not of hostility; one of union not of separation.'[45] For this reason, while the ideal tory could welcome an ascendancy of virtue and intellect, he could have nothing to do with the selfish ruling groups of the day, or with the Tory party as presently constituted. Mill welcomed the passage of the Reform Bill. He noted with satisfaction that the 'Tory party, at least the present Tory party, is now utterly annihilated. Peace be with it. All its elevated character had long gone out of it, and instead of a Falkland it had but a Croker, instead of a Johnson nothing better than a Philpotts'.[46] Also, while the ideal tory should obviously advocate unity and welcome agreement, this had to be a unity of conviction and genuine sympathy deriving from free inquiry. People should not be compelled into agreements they had neither felt nor experienced. They should come to common truths in their own way and in their own time. Ultimately they would agree, but only when they were ready to do so. In Mill's view, agreement was the result of common experiences and this one fact determined the methodological requirements of political philosophy.

In the essay 'On the Definition of Political Economy', for instance, an essay first written in the autumn of 1831 and then rewritten in the summer of 1833, 'with no immediate purpose of publication', Mill placed the recognition of common purposes at the very centre of political inquiry. He acknowledged that the study of man might proceed 'under several distinct hypotheses'.[47] Man could be taken to be a solitary individual, an individual coming into contact with other individuals, or an individual living in society. Mental philosophy worked on the first hypothesis, moral philosophy on the second and political philosophy on the third. Mental philosophy, or the study of man as a solitary individual, was only a preliminary consideration in morals and politics because it was solely concerned with 'the laws of the mere intellect, and those of the purely self-regarding desires'. Moral philosophy, in contrast, was concerned with those laws of human nature which related to the feelings called forth in individuals by other individuals, 'namely, the affections, the conscience, or feeling of duty, and the love of approbation'. Political philosophy, in turn, concerned those laws of feeling generated in man by living in a social state; 'that is, by forming part of a union or aggregation of human beings for a common purpose or purposes'.[48] There is some ambiguity in this definition. Obviously, the words 'union' and 'aggregation' have rather different connotations, but the general argument is straightforward enough. Philosophical inquiry into the nature of politics began with the supposition of a purpose or purposes common to all individuals in a society. The Benthamite idea of political man, as solely a rational calculator of self-regarding interest or desire, was at best a preliminary consideration. Man was more than a bundle of wants and aversions. The important fact in politics was the possession of common feelings and common sympathies, and whatever was predicated of the solitary individual and the single intellect, the social union itself was explicable only by reference to common purpose or purposes.

In one obvious sense, of course, this high-minded toryism emphasising shared feelings and common purposes was only as strong as Mill's eclecticism. Possibly it would be best interpreted as the appropriate political stance for an eclectic. Agreement rather than controversy, steady practice rather than doctrinal purity and a sympathetic tolerance in place of the narrowness of sect and party, all of these tory priorities or values were perfectly compatible with the eclectic disposition. They certainly fitted very well with the tolerant and comprehensive outlook Mill was so desperately seeking. He had no desire to return to the certainties of system, and the inclination to be tory expressed this fully. 'If I am asked what system of political philosophy I substituted for that which, as a philosophy, I had abandoned, I answer, no system: only a conviction, that the true system was something much more complex and many sided than I had previously had any idea of.'[49] There were also the accidents of personal contiguity. Mill was almost certain to regard toryism and eclecticism as natural allies because the tories he knew personally were also considered to be the best examples of eclecticism. Wordsworth, Coleridge and Southey had avoided sectarianism and militancy. They had ridiculed the dogmas of commonplace politicians. Their cultivated attachment to individual self-improvement, to love of country and to the betterment of national character also gave them undeniably wide sympathies. Indeed, this concern for the nation and for the elaboration of a general philosophy of human culture capable of commanding broad agreement, was precisely what brought toryism and eclecticism so close together. Mill gave his considered view on this in 1840 in the essay on 'Coleridge'. A 'Tory philosopher', Mill wrote, 'cannot be wholly a Tory, but must often be a better Liberal than Liberals themselves; while he is the natural means of rescuing from oblivion truths which Tories have forgotten, and which the prevailing schools of Liberalism never knew'.[50]

To Mill the conclusion was obvious: no true eclectic need be ashamed of being tory; a disposition to the one implied an attachment to the other. And as we have suggested throughout this chapter, once Mill had committed himself against the fatalism of 'Philosophic Necessity' and to the activities of self-culture, his own recrimination at the past forced a further commitment to an eclectic and high-minded tory stance. He was led well away from the censorious and waspish temperament of radicalism. Now he was concerned with answerable questions, preferring to skirt contentious issues and to eschew grand theories. He was the complete pragmatist in fact, handling issues as they arose and always looking to extend the limits of practical compromise on the basis of commonsense maxims. This is the 'early' Mill about whom so very little has been written: a philosopher who sought agreement by avoiding principles; an individual who treated controversy with disdain and a thinker increasingly liable to present consensus as the indispensable condition for a free and virtuous society.

Notes Chapter I

1 Stillinger (ed.), *Autobiography* (London, O.U.P., 1971), p. 84.

2 ibid., p. 88.

3 ibid., p. 85. The passage of the *Memoirs* which so moved Mill was that in which Marmontel's father died and his young son was seized with inspiration. The psychological implications of this, touching repressed death-wishes and guilt-transference, have often been written about, sometimes with ludicrous conclusions. One fairly balanced interpretation of a supposedly 'classical Oedipal situation' is Gertrude Himmelfarb, *On Liberty and Liberalism* (New York, Alfred Knopf, 1974). The first in the field, however, was A. W. Levi, 'The "Mental Crisis" of John Stuart Mill', *Psychoanalytic Review*, vol. XXXII, 1945, pp. 86–101.

4 *Autobiography*, op. cit., p. 85.

5 Our phrase is taken from James Mill, *Analysis of the Phenomena of the Human Mind* (London, Longmans et al., 1869), vol. 1, ch. 2, p. 52. The main ideas involved in this kind of radical empiricism are broadly surveyed in J. H. Randall, jr, *The Career of Philosophy* (New York, Columbia Univ. Press, 1965), ch. 7, in particular. But also see R. S. Peters (ed.), *Brett's History of Psychology* (London, George Allen & Unwin, 1953) and the old-fashioned but eminently sensible, H. C. Warren, *A History of the Association Psychology* (London, Constable & Co., 1921). There is, however, no general or systematic study which relates nineteenth-century philosophies of mind to philosophies of politics.

6 Quoted in René Wellek, *Immanuel Kant in England, 1793–1838* (Princeton, Univ. Press, 1931), p. 82. The same criticism using very similar imagery is made in *Biographia Literaria*, vol. 1, ch. 7. On Coleridge's response to the doctrines of associationism and empiricism, see R. L. Brett, *S. T. Coleridge: Writers and their Background* (London, Bell & Sons, 1971), and Humphrey House, *Coleridge, The Clark Lectures, 1951–52* (London, Rupert Hart-Davis, 1969), in particular ch. VI, pp. 142f. There is also an interesting essay by Dorothy Emmet in K. Coburn (ed.), *Coleridge, a collection of Critical Essays* (New Jersey, Prentice Hall, 1967). One might also add that Coleridge himself experienced a deep sense of despair when confronted by the doctrine of philosophical necessity: see *Collected Letters* (Oxford, E. L. Griggs, 1956), vol. II, p. 706.

7 W. H. Burston (ed.), *James Mill on Education* (Cambridge, Univ. Press ,1969), Section 1, p. 52.

8 *Autobiography*, op. cit., p. 74.

9 ibid., p. 44.

10 ibid., p. 101.

11 ibid., p. 102.

12 ibid., p. 86.

13 There is a vast, untidy and rather unreliable literature on this subject. I. W. Mueller, *John Stuart Mill and French Thought* (Urbana, Illinois Univ. Press, 1956), is massively detailed with a tendency to naïvity. R. K. P. Pankhurst, *The Saint-Simonians, Mill and Carlyle* (London, Sigdwick & Jackson, 1957), is very readable, but it was published before full use could be made of Mill's correspondence and is rather casual in some of its judgements. For the specialists, there is Dwight Lindley, *The Saint-Simonians, Carlyle and Mill*, Ph.D. thesis, Columbia Univ. 1958.

14 Mill to d'Eichthal, *The Earlier Letters of John Stuart Mill, 1812–1848* (Toronto, Univ. of Toronto Press, 1963), *Collected Works*, vol. XII, pp. 41–2.

15 John Stuart Mill, 'Comparison of the Tendencies of French and English Intellect', *Monthly Repository*, vol. VII, Nov. 1833, p. 803. Like most of Mill's writings at this time, authorship was under an initial. For validation of authorship of this and other articles, see *Bibliography of the Published Writings of John Stuart Mill* (New York, AMS Press, 1970), a bibliography jointly compiled by N. MacMinn, J. R. Hainds and J. M. McCrimmon from one of Mill's notebooks.

16 Mill to d'Eichthal, *Letters*, op. cit., XII, p. 36.

17 ibid., p. 43.

18 'Comparison of the Tendencies of French and English Intellect', op. cit., p. 803.

19 'Notes' is slightly misleading in this context. Much of the speech was written out in full, ready for delivery; only parts are in the form of notes. The 'notes' are reprinted in Edward Alexander, *John Stuart Mill: Literary Essays* (Indianapolis, Bobbs-Merrill, 1967), Appendix: 'Wordsworth and Byron', pp. 343–55. Some of the notes, as well as a commentary on them, can be found in Karl Britton, 'J. S. Mill: A Debating Speech on Wordsworth, 1829', *Cambridge Review*, vol. LXXIX, March 1958, pp. 418–23.

20 Mill kept a journal of this walking tour. As far as I know, this has not been published. For details and information see, Anna J. Mill, 'John Stuart Mill's Visit to Wordsworth, 1831', *Modern Language Review*, vol. XLIV, 1949, pp. 341–50. As the author points out, it is very likely that Mill first met Wordsworth before the tour at one of Henry Taylor's breakfasts.

21 Mill to Sterling, *Letters*, op. cit., XII, pp. 80–1.

22 ibid., p. 205. The early draft of the *Autobiography*, written in the winter of 1853–4, was very explicit about this extreme and benevolent tolerance. See *Autobiography*, op. cit., note to p. 105: 'I did not judge or criticize at all'.

23 J. S. Mill (anon.), 'Use and Abuse of Political Terms', *Tait's Edinburgh Magazine*, vol. I, May 1832, pp. 164–72. This contains a lively defence of 'state of nature' and 'social compact' arguments used by Locke and Rousseau.

24 Mill to Carlyle, *Letters*, op. cit., XII, p. 205.

25 J. S. Mill (anon.), 'Blakey's History of Moral Science', *Monthly Repository*, vol. VII, Oct. 1833, pp. 661–9. We should note the eclectic conclusion: 'The grand consideration is, not what any person regards as the ultimate end of human conduct, but through what intermediate ends he holds that his ultimate end is attainable' (p. 669).

26 Mill to d'Eichthal, *Letters*, op. cit., XII, pp. 45–6.

27 *Autobiography*, op. cit., p. 94.

28 *Westminster Review*, April 1828, p. 252.

29 Mill to Sterling, *Letters*, op. cit., XII, p. 78.

30 ibid., p. 101.

31 *Autobiography*, op. cit., p. 95.

32 Mill to Comte, *Letters*, op. cit., XIII, p. 489.

33 Karl Britton, op. cit., p. 420.

34 J. S. Mill (anon.), 'Letter from an Englishman to a Frenchman on a recent Apology', *Monthly Repository*, vol. VIII, June 1834, pp. 394–5.

35 *Examiner*, 4 July 1832, p. 450. J. H. Burns makes very considerable use of these two articles in his account of the development of Mill's views on democracy. See 'J. S. Mill and Democracy, 1829–1861' in J. B. Schneewind, *Mill: A Collection of Critical Essays* (London, Macmillan & Co., 1969), pp. 280–328.

36 J. S. Mill, 'The Rationale of Political Representation', *London and Westminster Review*, vol. 1 and 30 (*L.R.* 1, *W.R.* XXX), July 1835, pp. 347–8. For an elaboration of Mill's arguments on Prussia, Prussian government and the aristocratic principle see, 'Mrs. Austin's Translation of M. Cousin's Report on the State of Public Instruction in Prussia', *Monthly Repository*, vol. VIII, July 1834, pp. 502–13. The Austins were obviously decisive in building up Mill's admiration for Prussia.

37 *Autobiography*, op. cit., p. 38; and see also pp. 106–7. Mill kept his early tory fondness for generalising about national character throughout his life, and he regularly presented the English as dull, unimaginative and rather sordid people. See, for instance, Mill's Diary, Appendix A, Hugh Elliot (ed.), *The Letters of John Stuart Mill* (London, Longmans et al., 1910), vol. II, pp. 357–86, in particular the entries for 9 March and 5 April. One is reminded of Marx's aphorism in *The Poverty of Philosophy*: if the German transforms hats into ideas, 'the Englishman transforms men into hats'.

38 These articles are reprinted in several places. We have used J. B. Schneewind (ed.), *Mill's Essays on Literature and Society* (New York, Collier-Macmillan, 1965), pp. 27–78. The articles themselves have been the subject of considerable controversy, notably on the question of their indebtedness to Saint-Simonian philosophy. A useful guide to the literature of this controversy can be found in R. B. Friedman, 'An Introduction to Mill's Theory of Authority', in Schneewind, *Mill: A Collection of Critical Essays*, op. cit., pp. 379–425. Mill's own response to these articles can be found in the *Autobiography*, p. 104. These are the articles, of course, which Carlyle read and then said to himself, 'Here is a new Mystic'. Soon after this, Carlyle met Mill personally when he visited London from Craigenputtock to arrange for the publication of *Sartor Resartus*.

39 'The Spirit of the Age', J. B. Schneewind (ed.), *Mill's Essays*, op. cit., p. 46.

40 Mill wrote this anonymous commentary at the request of Edward Lytton Bulwer. Contrary to expectation, it was reprinted *ipsissimis verbis* as Appendix B in Bulwer's *England and the English* (Paris, 1834), pp. 376–88. My quotation is from the edition in *Essays on Ethics, Religion and Society* (Toronto, Univ. of Toronto Press, 1969), *Collected Works*, vol. X, p. 9. Mill also wrote a commentary on his father, but the ms. was so altered by Bulwer that he would not acknowledge authorship.

41 Mill to Sterling, *Letters*, op. cit., XII, pp. 83–4.

42 There are several examples of this kind of interpretation. The best known is probably Maurice Cowling, *Mill and Liberalism* (Cambridge, Univ. Press, 1963). But H. J. McCloskey also interprets Mill in this way, see *John Stuart Mill: A Critical Study* (London, Macmillan & Co., 1971). S. R. Letwin, *The Pursuit of Certainty* (London, Cambridge Univ. Press, 1965) also inclines to this interpretation, though in a less obvious fashion.

43 Mill to Martineau, *Letters*, op. cit., XII, p. 264. See also Mill to Tait, *The Later Letters of John Stuart Mill, 1849–1873* (Toronto, Univ. of Toronto Press, 1972), *Collected Works*, vol. XVII, Appendix 1: Additional Early Letters, pp. 1962–3.

44 Mill to Sterling, *Letters*, op. cit., XII, p. 76.

45 'Coleridge', *Essays on Ethics, Religion and Society*, op. cit., p. 135.

46 Mill to Carlyle, *Letters*, op. cit., XII, p. 106.

47 *Essays on Economics and Society* (Toronto, Univ. of Toronto Press, 1967), *Collected Works*, vol. IV, p. 319.

48 ibid., p. 320.

49 *Autobiography*, op. cit., p. 97.

50 'Coleridge', op. cit., pp. 162–3.

Chapter II

Romantic and Utilitarian

Many of the eclectic and tory themes we have been examining have obvious intellectual origins. They were sparked off by the romantic movement and by the idealist critique of materialism and sensationalism. They were, in fact, part of a deep-seated contempt for the whole 'mechanico-corpuscular' philosophy: part of that very general reaction against the dogmatic, disputatious and sectarian nature of old-fashioned radicalism; a radicalism commonly associated with the French disruption of the *ancien régime* and with the optimistic secularism of the European enlightenment. Perhaps one ought not to talk of the romantic movement at all. The definite article hardly seems excusable when there was no single idealist response. There was also no organisation, no leader and no 'official' romantic opinion. Consequently, no one is confident nowadays, either in talking of a Lakes school, or in postulating a coherent romantic philosophy. This is probably sensible, particularly when one is dealing with an ambience of thought and not with a methodical doctrine. Even so, the antithesis between analysis and imagination, between intellect and feeling and between the mind and some more inward and delicate sensibility, an antithesis used time and time again to reject the 'steam intellect' society, to ridicule its acquisitive philosophy and to scorn radicalism, was a reality in Mill's own experience. He lived with this antithesis, and his reading of Wordsworth, Coleridge and Shelley, as well as of de Vigny and Novalis, confirmed an opposition between science and poetry and between reason and the feelings which seemed peculiarly appropriate to himself. The breakdown had pointed to varieties of knowledge and experience completely outside the solely rational and analytic exercises of his youth. Moreover, his open and eclectic stance only served to confirm the deficiencies of rationalism.

In Mill's view, many-sidedness, which was the motto of Goethe and the crucial eclectic virtue, would be either unlikely or impossible if reason alone were relied upon. Rational analysis was far too limited for eclectic purposes. The true eclectic felt what others had felt; he imagined situations he had not directly encountered. Knowledge was a kind of alert and active experience, making sensitivity, not analysis,

44

indispensable. A solely rational acquaintance with the opinions and attitudes of others, even if it were feasible, would only be a nodding acquaintance: a dull, uninspired and merely formal point of contact, inferior in all respects to a shared experience. As Mill explained in his rambling review of Tennyson's poetry, the faculty of 'bringing home to us a coherent conception of beings unknown to our experience, not by logically *characterising* them, but by a living *representation* of them, is what is meant by creative imagination'.[1] None of the romantics could possibly have disagreed with this. And like the romantics, Mill was fairly certain of the danger: a bare-faced meanness of attitude, a pedantic narrowness of spirit, would defeat everything; no amount of reasoning and no degree of analytic activity would be sufficient protection against this. While 'a good mental discipline' might well be effective 'against false premises and unsound reasoning', it would be 'a very imperfect protection against the dangers of overlooking something'.[2] There is no real problem in interpreting this. As an eclectic and high-minded tory, Mill had come round to the view that knowledge required a kind of heightened awareness; a level of personal experience in which the feelings and the sentiments were crucial. There could be no tolerant and no comprehensive philosophy without a variety of emotional experiences. The mind would remain fixed, passively running through its humdrum operations, totally inert and completely without imagination. Whether this is characteristically 'romantic' or not, whether the belief was quite as coherent as we have suggested, it was certainly very different from the view that Mill had been brought up with.

No matter the particular emphases and the nuances they imparted, all of the Benthamites adopted paradigms of knowledge derived from the sciences of nature. They were unremitting positivists. Knowledge was strictly equated with the methods of science: with factual or non-evaluative observation and experiment; with the deduction of necessary connections ordering observable phenomena and with the discovery of exact laws. This was Newtonian science as they understood it; a combination of mathematical deduction with empirical observation. All else was mere speculation and mysticism. Consequently, the Benthamites took the sentiments and feelings of the individual observer to be irrelevant at best. They made no difference to the truth or falsity of propositions. Indeed, the language of the feelings was characteristically inexact, illogical and untidy, while the sentiments were a hindrance to objectivity and likely to make impartiality impossible. The Benthamites were also suspicious of the imagination. It made no regular and testable assertions about empirical reality, being indistinguishable from absurd flights of fancy. In short, there was an antipathy between poetry and truth and between feeling and reason built into the core of science.

Objective knowledge demanded the absolute exclusion of personal feelings. Mill had no difficulty in recalling this positivist distrust of emotion and feeling; it was so much a part of the whole ethos of Benthamism, and in the *Autobiography*, he presented Roebuck and his father as typical of the school. Roebuck, for instance, responded to the presence of feelings with a lumpish and awkward embarrassment. One would be far better off without them.[3] His father, on the other hand, 'thought that feeling could take care of itself'. He had, Mill explained, 'a real impatience of attributing praise to feeling, or of any but the most sparing reference to it either in the estimation of persons, or in the discussion of things'.[4] James Mill, in fact, considered modern times less moral than ancient times because of the great stress laid on feeling. John Mill himself was very uneasy about this attitude. His breakdown had made indifference to feeling seem a rather dangerous fallacy, and just as he had turned against his previous radicalism, so he also began to turn against a strictly positivist conception of knowledge. More and more, he objected to any attempt to confine 'knowledge' or 'truth' solely to empirical operations analogous to those in the sciences of nature.

The first clear signs of this shift away from positivism can be seen in Mill's attempts to distinguish poetic natures from other natures, to define the uniqueness of the poetic mind and to establish poetry as a reputable pursuit. The defence of Wordsworth in 1829 was an obvious beginning, and after that a commitment to poetry became essential to Mill's notion of culture. Like Coleridge, he saw poetry as both an ideal vision and a moral habit without which no man was complete. He returned to these notions again and again in the early years of the thirties, attempting to make sense of several distinctions only recently familiar to him. The basic distinctions are fairly clear, though the details of his argument are more complex than we can suggest here. In a mind without any strong feelings, a mind which was also entirely uncultivated, thought simply reflected the chronology of events. The mind copied sensations as circumstances dictated, acting as a passive instrument of the environment. The 'thread of association' was successive, casual and easily broken. With the scientific or business mind, on the other hand, the objects of experience were firmly ranked and ordered, being put in their place by the understanding. Here, the associations were grouped and classified 'for the convenience of thought or of practice'. The poetic mind was different from both of these. With this mind, all images and all thoughts referred to a feeling. 'All the combinations which the mind puts together, all the pictures which it paints, all the wholes which Imagination constructs out of the materials supplied by Fancy, will be indebted to some dominant *feeling*, not as in other natures to a dominant thought.'[5] In poetry, the rational faculty was only a medium for the expression of feeling, while the understanding itself was shaped by sentiments and not by circumstances.

These distinctions may seem rather contrived, a little too carefully fashioned, perhaps, to be entirely convincing. There is also a marked secondhand quality about them, but Mill was primarily concerned to break with the positivist ethos. He denied that strong feeling or passionate emotion made the truth impossible. Strong feeling did not bias judgement. Passionate emotion was perfectly consistent with great calmness. Indeed, he now believed the 'capacity for strong feeling' to be 'the material out of which all *motives* are made; the motives, consequently, which lead human beings to the pursuit of truth'. Self-culture demanded energy of character and 'energy of character is always the offspring of strong feeling'.[6] Whatever its standing as literary theory and no matter the sources, this argument made poetry indispensable to moral improvement. Poetry and the poetic mind, as Mill now emphasised, had the 'noble end' of 'acting upon the desires and characters of mankind through their emotions, to raise them towards the perfection of their nature'.[7] Poetry was a part of man's progressiveness, not a silly and unnecessary indulgence as the Benthamites had so obviously believed. It was these beliefs about poetry and about the poetic mind which confirmed Mill's doubts about the efficacy of reason and the dominance of the rational faculty. More than ever before, he was inclined to relate inquiry to poetry and to argue the need for a general philosophy of human culture based upon the cultivation of feeling.

Some care is needed, however. The past was not obliterated by these new concerns, and Mill was always prepared to admit the possibility of acting upon the mind and of directing conduct by the formation of exclusively rational associations of pain and pleasure. Men acted rationally when they calculated the balance of hedonistic consequences. There was also no doubt that the objects of experience could be ordered by reason as the tilt of pleasure and pain required, but while not doubting these psychological facts and their relevance to mental philosophy, Mill still worried about the consequences. In his view, such associations were artificial and casual. They tended to be weak and irregular, lacking those complements and correctives which associations could derive from a 'natural tie' in the emotions. In the long run, in fact, the immediate associations of pain and pleasure tended to deaden the spirit and 'to wear away the feelings'.[8] Responses certainly became more predictable, but they also became much less sensitive and much less flexible. So, although solely rational groupings or clusters of associations were favourable to prudence and to clear-sightedness, qualities very welcome to both the scientific and the business mind, they were also 'a perpetual worm at the root both of the passions and of the virtues'. In effect, Mill now took the associations involved with the moral feeling and with all strong feelings in general, to be natural rather than mechanical. They were rooted in the emotions rather than the will, in the affections rather than the appetites. This is a significant departure from the orthodoxies of psychological hedonism, and it explains Mill's savagery in dealing with Sedgwick's moral philosophy in the middle thirties. Utilitarians did not take the moral feelings to be 'factitious and artificial associations'. On the contrary, Mill remarked coldly, 'the best teachers of the theory of utility' took them to be a fact of man's natural constitution: 'the idea of the pain of another is naturally painful; the idea of the pleasure of another is naturally pleasurable'.[9]

This emphasis on the natural, the organic and the emotional has often been ridiculed. Commentators tend to write about it with a touch of sarcasm. Perhaps Mill himself is to blame. He often wrote with a wide-eyed innocence while expressing the most mundane and hackneyed of sentiments. There is undoubtedly an air of clumsy bucolicism about his early exercises in romantic epistemology, but the intention is still perfectly clear. However clumsily, Mill was attempting to minimise the case for reason and the rational faculty, and his propositions were simple but significant. Intellectual culture needed to be balanced by emotional culture. Analysis was sure to be insufficient by itself. Poetic truth was also needed to reveal ideals capable of inspiring conduct and of improving character. If these beliefs were naïve, derivative and rather poorly expressed, they were also very persistent. As late as 1848, over twenty years after the crisis, it was possible for Mill to write to Pringle Nichol informing him that the great merit of Comte's *Discours sur l'ensemble du Positivisme* was 'the systematic and earnest inculcation of the purely *subordinate* role of the intellect as the minister of the higher sentiments'.[10] Here again was the authentic voice of the romantic protesting against the whole course of eighteenth-century materialism.

What had happened to Mill was clear. The crisis had provoked a shift in his epistemology. He now accepted a necessary connection between self-consciousness, emotional sensitivity and knowledge. He had drawn away from the positivist ideal. Non-evaluative observation would bring neither insight nor awareness, and rational judgement was a form of defective or incomplete experience. Like all romantics, Mill regarded suffering as the price to be paid for knowledge at all out of the ordinary. The tortured self-conscious which experienced deep feeling was the demon of all modern men of genius; to know was to suffer. In fact, he was inclined to interpret his own breakdown in just this fashion. The 'gloom and morbid despondency', after all, had produced 'all the most valuable of such insight as I have into the most important matters'.[11] Consequently, he now believed that knowledge could not be taught.

Being a kind of intense experience, a form of personal awareness, there were no rules or techniques of discovery to be passed from one generation to another. Only a mind which had actively studied itself, painfully learning by introspection, was capable of that order of experience which brought true knowledge. Whatever such a view supposed about the organisation of the mind and about possible differences between minds, the didactic Benthamite stress on instruction, learning and teaching was entirely inappropriate. Man would not become good by being taught opinions. Knowledge was not a consequence of teaching at all. The end of education, Mill explained, very much in the style of Coleridge and Shelley, was not to teach 'but to fit the mind for learning from its own consciousness and observation'. To know a truth was always to discover it for oneself. 'Knowledge comes only from within; all that comes from without is but *questioning*, or else it is mere *authority*.'[12] The positivist ideal had been left a long way behind. The validity of knowledge now rested upon its ability to stand the test of personal reflection.

This idea of knowledge as personal experience carried many implications. Sensation would seem to precede judgement, while judgement itself, like experience, could never be complete. One might also properly suppose a kind of inner and intuitive truth beyond logical demonstration and empirical proof. Mill did not dodge this implication. He informed Carlyle, for instance, that 'most of the highest truths' were truths of this kind. Certainly he no longer believed truth to be an artefact or entity which could be promoted by public examination, or extracted from the cognitive process by the imposition of rewards and punishments. 'Truth is *sown* and germinates in the mind itself and is not to be struck *out* suddenly like fire from a flint by knocking another hard body against it.'[13] The very opposite was the case. The truth would prove itself at the end of a long day of suffering. As Mill reminded d'Eichthal, 'no good seed is lost: it takes root and springs up somewhere, and will help in time towards the general reconstruction of the opinions of the civilized world, for which ours is only a period of preparation'. 'Therefore, "cast ye your bread on the waters, and ye shall find it after many days".'[14] Presumably, this explains why Mill once remarked that he 'would most gladly postulate like Kant a different ultimate foundation "*subjectiver bedürfnisses willen*" if I could'.[15]

There is no doubt at all, then, that by the end of the twenties and the beginning of the thirties, Mill had turned away from a rigorous and analytic positivism towards a romantic and idealist stance, and any consideration of his utilitarianism has to accept this as a matter of fact. He now presumed the uniqueness of the poetic mind. He refused to see an antagonism between poetry and truth. Imaginative emotion made strong character and strong character was indispensable to good moral and political conduct. Part of the attractiveness of the French nation, for example, was their habit of uniting politics and poetry. With the prosaic English, this was wholly exceptional; to be seen only 'in the great poetic figures', in 'a Shelley, a Byron, or a Wordsworth'. Mill himself was clear about the change and when it had taken place. He believed his separation from the Benthamite school of radicals had first been made public in 1829. His defence of Wordsworth at the London Debating Society was the crucial event. After that, the separation became wider and wider as time went on. He chided Albany Fonblanque for not recognising this, at the same time refusing to be identified 'with Grote, Roebuck or the rest'.[16] Most of his friends and close contemporaries did not need reminding, however. To Carlyle and Place, Mill had become a 'mystic'. To John Bowring he was 'a renouncer of Bentham's creed and an expounder of Coleridge's'.[17] Mrs Grote, apparently, adopted the habit of referring to Mill either as 'the Lama' or as that 'wayward intellectual deity'; neither was particularly complimentary. Morley remembered Mill recalling how angry his former radical friends had been at his new-found love for Wordsworth.[18] As I hope to have shown, in at least three areas or aspects, these contemporary judgements were substantially correct. In analytic psychology, political philosophy and epistemology Mill had ceased to be a Benthamite. He had become, instead, an eclectic fellow traveller of the romantics, sharing the salient points of their critique of enlightenment rationalism. Coleridge was undoubtedly influential in this. Mill wrote to Pringle Nichol that 'few persons have exercised more influence over my thoughts and character than Coleridge has'. Coleridge was 'the most systematic thinker of our time'; 'without excepting even Bentham, whose edifice is as well bound together, but is constructed on so much simpler a plan, and covers so much less ground. On the whole, there is more food for thought—and the best kind of thought—in Coleridge than in all other contemporary writers'.[19]

We should be careful not to be misled, however. As an eclectic, Mill did not feel that he had to choose finally between rationalism and romanticism. He could combine a poetic toryism with an intense romanticism and still remain a utilitarian. This is not a semantic point. Mill never wavered in the belief that the ultimate end or criterion of human action was what human beings desired; this was a fixed point in his thinking. His assimilation of knowledge to personal experience was not taken to invalidate the methods of observation and induction, and he always resisted any attempt to make moral judgement a matter of direct perception and not of reasoning. More than anything else, possibly, this was due to Mill's *simpliste* understanding of philosophical allegiance and to his division of philosophy into the *a posteriori* and the *a priori* schools. Ultimately, he thought, the philosopher was either an Aristotelian or a Platonist. The philosophy of experience could not be reconciled with the philosophy of intuition and no philosopher could honestly hold to both at the same time. So while he was bound to acknowledge that his idea of utility was exceptional and idiosyncratic, needing 'an immense number and variety of explanations', Mill never took himself to be rejecting utilitarianism.[20] This was true even at the high point of his reaction against Benthamism. Mill remained a philosopher of experience, taking the utilitarian principle to be an essential part of the experiential philosophy. Without the principle, the methods of observation, analysis and induction would be severely restricted in scope: knowledge would be confused with custom and habit; and all claims to objective assessment in morals and politics would have to be abandoned. This was a consistent position to adopt, quite compatible with all the shifts we have outlined, but it did require one special assumption; that Benthamism was not synonymous with a true utilitarianism. Mill could only maintain his combination of romanticism and rationalism by rejecting Bentham's hedonistic utilitarianism.

Indeed, after the crisis, Mill felt obliged to re-educate the philosophical public on just this point. After all, the popular conception of the Benthamite as a cold, doctrinaire man of system was not too far from the truth. As it stood, Benthamism had damaged the philosophy of experience by linking it with too narrow an idea of human nature and with too stipulative a definition of truth. Benthamism had also ceased to be instrumental in political reforms, making no improvements in national character. In Mill's view, there was an obvious need to distinguish a true utilitarian doctrine from the merely prudential hedonism which had become fashionable. This was particularly so amongst the English, who were only too happy to regard morals and politics as extentions of trade. Once the crisis was over, this became a major concern. The public was to be re-educated with a new utilitarianism. Obviously, the new variant would have to retain the traditional animus against intuitionism and against the *a priorism* of the German metaphysicians but in separating itself from Benthamism and in moving a little closer to romanticism, utilitarianism would become more appropriate to the day and age, better able to serve as a philosophy of improvement. The utilitarian principle would cease to be narrow, dogmatic and doctrinaire. Consequently, more and more people would be able to agree with it. The principle would then serve a real eclectic function, bringing people together and ending the antagonisms promoted by the Benthamites. Mill explained his new attitude to Edward Lytton Bulwer, in an attempt to recruit him as a writer for the *London and Westminster Review*. There is no better short statement of romantic utilitarianism. Mill explained that a broad and tolerant philosophy was being sought: 'one which takes into account the whole of human nature not the ratiocinative faculty only'. There would be no sectarianism. Utilitarians should fraternise 'with all who hold the same *axiomata media* (as Bacon has it) whether their first principle is the same or not—and which holds in the highest reverence all which the vulgar notion of utilitarians represents them to despise—which holds Feeling at least as valuable as Thought, and Poetry not only on a par with, but the necessary condition of, any true and comprehensive Philosophy'.[21]

At the time when Mill was making this distinction between Benthamism and true utilitarianism, using his new language of romanticism, he was also rediscovering an interest in radicalism.[22] This did not happen overnight. His quiet and contemplative toryism was very persistent, and the spirit of eclecticism prevented a return to the hotheaded commitments of his youth. But his quietism, at least, began to give way. Mill became much less reticent about public affairs and party causes. He wrote about them, talked about them: politics had become interesting again. This was most noticeable, perhaps, after the passage of the Reform Bill in 1832. The Tory party seemed to be finished, while the success of radical candidates in the elections of 1832 was very encouraging. Grote was returned for the City of London and Roebuck for Bath. 'I must not desert them but give them such help as lies in me.'[23] In July 1833, in a letter to John Sterling, Mill made a clean breast of his increasing commitment, using the occasion to point to a difference between them. 'I think I am becoming *more* a Movement-man than I was, instead of less—I do not mean merely in politics, but in all things—and that you are becoming more and more inclined to look backward for good.'[24] The death of James Mill in 1836 may also have removed certain inhibitions, and Mill suggests this himself in the *Autobiography*. Although he had been deprived of his father's aid and assistance, 'I was also exempted from the restraints and reticences by which that aid had been purchased. I did not feel that there was any other radical writer or politician to whom I was bound to defer, further than consisted with my own opinions.'[25] Whatever the motivation, from the mid thirties Mill was working not only to separate Benthamism from utilitarianism, but also to reorganise the radical party and to free it from sectarianism. In his own mind, these were simply two aspects of the one aim: to create a better radical philosophy than Benthamism, a philosophy of movement rather than of expediency, for a new and revitalised reform party.

The essay on 'Civilization', published in the *London and Westminster Review*, and the review of the writings of Junius Redivivus published in the *Monthly Repository*, were the first attempts to sketch out this philosophy of movement and they show very clearly the continuing importance of the eclectic stance.[26] Indeed, radicalism seems to be eclecticism with the quietism removed. Like the eclectic, the radical was primarily an enemy to sectarianism. The common ambition was to overthrow dogmatism: sectarian teaching, the inculcation of narrow and limited opinions with no particular regard for their truth or falsity, should be ended altogether. 'The principle itself of dogmatic religion, dogmatic morality, dogmatic philosophy, is what requires to be rooted out; not any particular manifestation of that principle.' The radical, then, was bound to have a primary commitment to educational reform. But again like the eclectic, he had a low opinion of formal instruction. This shows quite clearly in Mill's view of the universities. 'As a means of educating the many', they were 'absolutely null'. They had produced few great scholars, and they still extracted the promise of belief in certain opinions by means of the Tests and other devices. The curriculum, in any case, was very poor. Only classics and mathematics were seriously encouraged, in 'moral and psychological science', there was 'the mere shell and husk of the syllogistic logic at the one', the 'wretchedest smattering of Locke and Paley at the other'. Given the condition of the universities and a general unease about formal instruction, the radicals' way to educational improvement could only be by social and political innovation. Although one or two individuals might be able to cultivate themselves and to enlarge their feelings in the present circumstances, no improvement was possible for the majority in the absence of social reform. Only the radicals had fully grasped this fact. So although 'the cultivation of the minds of the people is the source to which he looks exclusively for any sensible improvement in their well-being', the radical was also certain 'that anything deserving the name of universal cultivation will never be had until our social institutions are purified from the infection of jobbery and lying, which poisons all that would otherwise be good in them'.[27] Social and political reform was not optional but necessary. Education could not proceed effectively against sectarianism without it, while dogmatism would remain untroubled. Mill also saw some tactical advantages. No one doubted that the privileged classes would concede very little. But even these classes would realise they had more to fear from the poor when uneducated than when educated. They might become reluctant reformers in that respect at least.

But no matter what the tactical benefits of a policy of educational reform might be, the radical party could never be allied with privilege. As a party, it was compelled to oppose privilege in all its traditional guises, whether of aristocratic rule, middle-class materialism, or the dogmatism of the established church. Mill himself reserved a particular contempt for the landed aristocracy. They placed their incompetents in sinecures. They kept up the price of food by the Corn Laws. Their dominance in county politics maintained an attenuated feudalism in the countryside and kept intact a wholly false system of authority. Just as the 'moral basis of Toryism' was submission to rightful authority, so 'the moral basis of Radicalism is the refusal to pay that submission to an authority which is usurped, or to which the accidents of birth or fortune are the only title'.[28] Properly conceived, radicalism was opposed to all oligarchy, and the radical was by nature an inveterate enemy to all unjust deprivations:

> 'and to all institutions and all usages which deliver over any portion of the species, unprotected, to the tender mercies of any other portion; whether the sacrifice be of blacks to whites, of Catholics to Protestants, of the community at large to lords and borough-mongers, of the middle and working classes to the higher, of the working classes to the middle, or (a surer test of genuine high-minded radicalism than all the rest) of women to men'.[29]

Nevertheless, radicalism ought not to be confused with demagogic populism. Ignorance was ignorance, whether it was on the right side or not. The people were just as capable of irresponsible power as were the traditional oligarchs, particularly when so many of them were unable to make up their own minds for themselves. Knowledge, culture and experience were essential, and Mill was adamant that the true radical recognise 'that government is a work of nicety and difficulty, the subject of a peculiar science, requiring long study and appropriate intellectual culture'.[30] Not surprisingly, perhaps, Mill excluded universal suffrage from the radical programme. 'The motto of a Radical politician should be, Government *by means* of the middle for the working classes.' Mill, in fact, was quite taken by Edward Gibbon Wakefield's summary of the position in *England and America:* 'Until Universal Suffrage be possible, —to govern the country as it would be necessary to govern it, if there were Universal Suffrage and the people were well educated and intelligent.'[31] As a radical, Mill had remained true to at least some of his newly acquired toryism. If the landed aristocracy were incapable of inspired leadership, so also were the illiterate and nucultured masses.

Mill also hoped the radical party would be independent of the ministries and be led by Lord Durham. He advocated a complete separation from the Whigs, urging the radicals to move into an explicit and declared opposition. The lonely role of independent opposition in Parliament would be more than balanced by a broad popular appeal amongst the new electorate. The essay on the 'Reorganization of the Reform Party', which was written in 1838 but not published until the following year, shows the full extent of Mill's optimism; he might almost have been predicting consensus again on the basis of secondary maxims. Support would come from all of the 'disqualified classes': these were 'natural radicals'. There would also be support from the urban middle class, from small proprietors alienated by the landed interest, as well as from the Scots and the Irish. Above all, Mill assured his readers, the radicals could count on the working classes: 'classes deeply and increasingly discontented, and whose discontent now speaks out in a voice which will not be unheard'. No one would be excluded, however: the 'Reform party of the Empire ought not to be, cannot be, Radical in any narrow or sectarian sense'.[32] In the event, of course, Mill's general hopes as well as his particular efforts were disappointed. The radicals did not form an effective separate party, and they were far too high-minded to consider seriously acting as another distinct 'interest' in British politics; Lord Durham moreover would not commit himself. The political control of the Whigs and Tories in the reformed Parliament was never seriously challenged. Only one or two radicals sat for large and popular constituencies, and despite Mill's optimism about 'natural radicals', the party made no substantial gains amongst the new electorate. The 'movement party' was not a success and Mill more or less stopped working for it in 1839. He also gave up his ownership and effective editorship of the *London and Westminster Review* in the following year, announcing his general conclusions in a letter to Macvey Napier. There was simply no room in British politics for a fourth party, 'reckoning the Conservatives, the Whig-Radicals, and the Chartists as the other three'.[33] We are not concerned with the failure of the radical party as such; our interest is in Mill's utilitarianism as it was fashioned in these years of disappointed radicalism. Several obvious questions need answering: what was the new utilitarianism; how was it free from sectarianism, and in what sense, if at all, had it become distinct from Benthamism? Obvious questions, but not easy ones: we can begin to answer them by reminding ourselves of the issues the crisis had resolved.

Mill himself felt emancipated from simple psychological beliefs. Psychological hedonism, in particular, implied too neat and too narrow an account of motivation; there was no permanent human nature, to be explained by universal and invariant laws, the Saint-Simonians had been absolutely right in insisting on that. Mankind was not alike in all times and places. Rather than reduce motivation to uniform and primary sensations of pain and pleasure, Mill now preferred to follow Wordsworth in believing it possible to built up responses which transcended the immediate senses. In fact, the very attempt to list and to catalogue motives was, to his mind, misconceived; nothing about man was so fixed or final. 'Motives are innumerable: there is nothing whatever which may not become an object of desire or of dislike by association.'[34] Mill's 'theories of life', then, no longer presupposed the calculated pursuit and avoidance of pleasure and pain as an end or object. Habits of association were many and varied. And while happiness remained 'the test of all rules of conduct, and the end of life', 'those only are happy (I thought) who have their minds fixed on some object other than their own happiness'. The 'only chance is to treat, not happiness, but some end external to it, as the purpose of life'.[35] This has often been commented on: by a drastic act of surgery, Mill had detached utilitarianism from its basis in hedonism; the ethics of utility now claimed to be disinterested, and expediency was a thing of the past.

Mill also regarded as false and depressing those variants of associationism which presented the mind as passively determined by circumstance. Any view which suggested a person's character was made and fixed for him, either by nature or by the environment, ignored the real power of the will over motives, removed the consciousness of moral freedom and made it impossible to account for individual responsibility. Indeed, Mill now held a man to be free only to the extent that he had formed his own character as he would ideally wish it to be. 'And hence it is said with truth, that none but a person of confirmed virtue is completely free.'[36] Finally, there was also a marked loss of confidence in enlightened teaching and in formal instruction. Knowledge was a form of experience and could not be taught; far more would be gained by cultivating the affections and by broadening the emotions, making them more sensitive and more tolerant, than by correcting opinions and altering ideas. Imagination and sympathy were the crucial faculties: in their absence, there would only be the familiar didactic instruments of the Benthamites, praise and blame, reward and punishment. Like Austin, Mill now 'attached much less importance than formerly to outward changes, unless accompanied by a better cultivation of the inward nature'.[37]

All of these conclusions, about hedonism, about sensationalism and about self-determination, led Mill to relate moral philosophy to a philosophy of human culture much more closely than either Bentham or his father had ever considered possible. To Mill, a moral outlook was synonymous with a sympathetic interest in the common feelings and common destinies of all human beings. This coloured his views on the character of the moral feelings themselves. They were neither artificial nor mechanical, certainly not a mere accident of a particular balance of the sensations. They were part of man's makeup as a social creature: part of man as man, and with a universal basis in sympathy, which was the common factor of man's natural constitution. Mill explained this to William Ward, the catholic theologian. His language was plain and straightforward. The moral feeling was an internal as well as a disinterested feeling, existing 'quite independently of any expected consequences'. 'I conceive that feeling to be a natural outgrowth from the social nature of man.' This, when combined with man's 'capacity of fellow-feeling', was the ground of all moral conduct.[38] Consequently, in Mill's view, morality could never be a simple matter of teaching or instruction. He had learnt the romantic lesson: moral conduct required social awareness, and this, in turn, could result only from each person's own attempts at a culture in which imaginative sympathies were developed and made habitual. In effect, morality rested on acts of imagination, on leaps of awareness, which brought home the realities of social living. Each person had to transcend present desires in order to recognise the pleasures and pains of others; the ethics of utility could only be disinterested if this were the case. In some respects, of course, imagination and sympathy were identical qualities: Mill himself made little or no attempt to distinguish between them. Both involved an awareness and sharing of the feelings of others: both required a capacity to put oneself in another's place. Whatever the word, these were the qualities which made moral decisions possible. Further, all philosophies of morals required 'clear and comprehensive views of education and human culture'. Moral philosophy would not be understood 'but in proportion as the former is so'.[39] Indeed, the capacity for moral conduct, particularly for habitual moral conduct, demanded the highest development of human character. Mill insisted that all systems of ethics, all moral philosophies worthy of the name, should aid individuals 'in the formation of their own character', for just this reason.[40] We should now draw out one or two conclusions from these rather scattered remarks.

First, Mill should not be read as if he were a rule-utilitarian. Given the emphasis on self-education, on each person's making of his own character, the moral predicates 'right' and 'wrong' would not be applied to particular actions because those actions were either prescribed or proscribed by commonly accepted moral rules. The ethic of a true utilitarianism was one of self-development or self-realisation: self-culture not rational knowledge or mere learning, was indispensable. The test or proof of individual self-culture was not supplied by common rules, but by the extent to which each person voluntarily recognised obligations owed to other persons; this demonstrated his capacity for sympathetic imagination and made a reality of fellow-feeling. As Mill explained to Carlyle, the ultimate end of utilitarianism, which was 'the good of the species (or rather of its several units)', could 'in no other way be forwarded but by the means you speak of, namely by each taking for his exclusive aim the development of what is best in *himself*'.[41] This ethic of self-development gave rise to one simple injunction. If the good of all did require each person to develop himself, then everyone was obliged to form his character as he would ideally wish it to be. 'Try thyself unweariedly till thou findest the highest thing thou art capable of doing, faculties and outward circumstances being both duly considered—and then DO IT.'[42] Just as the mark of the eclectic was generous sympathy, so the mark of moral conduct was active self-improvement. The new utilitarianism simply extended the logic of self-culture to the reaches of moral philosophy.

Second, whatever else was implied by the new ethic of self-culture, the Benthamite understanding of the scope and application of moral judgements was now completely inadequate. Benthamism had been proud of its refusal to judge individual character, preferences and tastes; this was an unnecessary interference smacking of paternalism. Unless behaviour had specific other-regarding effects or consequences, consequences which could be observed and demonstrated, then it was of no concern to the moralist. A person's character as such was a matter of indifference; only his public or social conduct mattered. To talk of good or bad taste was mere dogmatism; there was liberty of taste, and the moralist had no right at all to pronounce on conduct which was neither good nor bad in its consequences for other people. The orthodoxy, indeed, was to make morality and law coterminous terms. Where the agent only was involved the matter was not a moral one, and the agent was not liable to praise and blame, to reward and punishment. To Mill, of course, this made self-culture unlikely and an adequate moral philosophy impossible. Knowledge of a person was bound to include an estimation of his tastes and preferences: this was how character was assessed. And Mill explicitly criticised Bentham for refusing to praise or to condemn in self-regarding areas:

'as if men's likings and dislikings, on things in themselves indifferent, were not full of the most important inferences as to every point of their character; as if a person's tastes did not show him to be wise or a fool, cultivated or ignorant, gentle or rough, sensitive or callous, generous or sordid, benevolent or selfish, conscientious or depraved'.[43]

Mill's argument was neither esoteric nor complex. Actions and character were indissolubly linked. The moral philosopher had to consider both together. In refusing to consider character, and in not including in the consequences of an act the consequences to the agent himself, Bentham had needlessly and wrongly limited the principle of utility to public conduct. He had 'largely exemplified, and contributed very widely to diffuse, a tone of thinking, according to which any kind of action or any habit, which in its own specific consequences cannot be proved to be necessarily or probably productive of unhappiness to the agent himself or to others, is supposed to be fully justified'.[44] The conclusion was obvious: moral judgement had to be judgement of person as well as of conduct, of character as well as of consequences.

The romantic influence may again be detected. The notion of self-culture had first been borrowed from Wordsworth. Coleridge had provided the association between morality, sympathy and imagination by insisting that the utilitarians of the eighteenth century had lacked 'sensibility'; a 'constitutional quickness of sympathy with pain and pleasure, and a keen sense of the gratifications that accompany social intercourse, mutual endearments, and reciprocal preferences'. Paley, in particular, had been at fault. In adopting 'the general consequences' doctrine, he had confused law and morality, drawing attention away from 'the inward motives and impulses which constitute the essence of morality'.[45] Mill adopted all of these views. Imagination, of course, was the faculty providing a 'constitutional quickness of sympathy'; for the imaginative person at least, the associations involved with the moral feeling were neither artificial nor mechanical. In his essay 'On Genius', Mill argued the romantic case directly. A man should be judged, 'not by what he does, but by what he is'. What mattered was the spirit in which a man performed his works rather than the works themselves. 'Nor is this mere mysticism; the most absolute utilitarianism must come to the same conclusion.'[46] In Mill's view, the moral philosopher had to consider the person and his inner character for one very good reason, for 'it often happens that an essential part of the morality or immorality of an action or a rule of action consists in its influence upon the agent's own mind: upon his susceptibilities of pleasure or pain, upon the general direction of his thoughts, feelings and imagination'.[47] The logic of this is clear. Without each individual's own attempt to cultivate himself and to develop an imaginative sympathy, desires would remain purely self-regarding. No attempt would be made to modify feelings with reference to the feelings of others. There would be no effective or permanent recognition of common purpose or purposes. Fellow-feeling would remain undeveloped. Morality would be limited to a few prudential forbearances. The '*petite morale*' alone would be considered 'and on the *quid pro quo* principles which regulate trade'.[48] It was for just this reason that all systems of ethics, all worthy moral philosophies, should endeavour to aid individuals in the formation of their own character. They had to be inspirational. Obviously, they would fail to be so if individual tastes and preferences were treated as matters of complete indifference. In effect, by following the romantics, Mill had extended the scope of moral judgement, and in his new utilitarianism, conduct which was neither good nor bad in its other-regarding consequences, might still be amenable to moral praise and blame in its self-regarding aspects.

Initially, extending the scope of moral concern to include the character of the agent as well as the consequences of an action to persons other than the agent, led Mill to divide morality into two equal and interdependent parts. The famous essay on 'Bentham' gave the clearest statement of this two-part theory. Here Mill insisted that the first part of morality was self-education: 'the training, by the human being himself, of his affections and will. That department is a blank in Bentham's system. The other and co-equal part, the regulation of his outward actions, must be altogether halting and imperfect without the first'.[49] Mill had clearly abandoned the idea that where the agent only was concerned the matter was not a moral one. His commitment to self-culture suggested there was a duty to improve oneself, the agent's concern for his own personal worth being an essential preparation for responsible social conduct. Without that preparation morality would be limited to a halting series of minimal forbearances. Paley had already reduced utilitarianism to a kind of prudential business ethic; Bentham had followed him by making law and morality coterminous terms. Both of these views ignored the moral part of man's nature 'in the strict sense of the term', 'the desire of perfection, or the feeling of an approving or an accusing conscience'.[50] As an eclectic, however, Mill was also concerned to avoid the pedantic narrowness of Benthamism. He became concerned with the 'error' or 'one-sidedness' involved 'in treating the moral view of actions and characters', as if it were the sole view. Not every question was a question of morality. All conduct could be approached in more ways than one and no true eclectic should possess only one standard for all varieties of experience. It was this concern which led Mill to add a rather more complex division of conduct towards the end of the essay on 'Bentham'. The two-part theory of morality was replaced by a three-fold division of conduct. Every human action, Mill maintained, had three aspects: 'its *moral* aspect, or that of its right and wrong; its *aesthetic* aspect, or that of its beauty; its sympathetic aspect, or that of its *lovableness*'.[51]

After the publication in 1838 of the essay on 'Bentham', Mill was increasingly inclined to neglect the two-part theory of morality in favour of this broader, more complex division of human conduct. One can easily see why. Part of the narrowness of Benthamism had to do with its dogmatic and moralising spirit. The philosophic radicals had ignored feeling, they had something close to contempt for poetry, and the varieties of conduct were of as little interest to them as the nuances of experience. Mill had to avoid all of this. So he began to elaborate a prescriptive philosophy of action, an 'Art of Life' as he called it in the

Logic, in which there was a three-fold division of conduct into morality, prudence and aesthetics, thus avoiding the two Benthamite categories of indifference and moral praise or blame. He was not always consistent in his usage; one might also wish he had written rather more on the division. What is said in the essay on 'Bentham', for instance, is not quite the same as the account given in the *Logic.* Usually, however, he adopted that division of conduct which placed self-education, the inner character, in the realms of prudence and aesthetics. And while he never suggested that the character of an individual was a matter of indifference, self-culture was not properly a part of morality. There was no moral duty to improve oneself and there could be no question of punishment for a lack of personal worth. At least, this is the view taken in most of the writings published after the 1838 essay: in *On Liberty,* for instance, Mill held that no self-regarding fault could properly be called immoral; presumably, no self-regarding virtue either was properly moral. Here, Mill would seem to have relinquished the two-part theory of morality quite decisively. Personal worth might well excite sympathy; people might also be attracted to the beauties of a developed character, and there could even be clear prudential grounds for embarking on self-education. But, despite all of this, the inner character was not to be judged in terms of moral praise or blame. The only point to be insisted on was that this was still no reason to be indifferent to character. All increases in human happiness due merely to a change of circumstances, unaccompanied 'by changes in the state of the desires', were hopeless. 'Not to mention,' Mill added, 'that while the desires are circumscribed in self', there could never be an adequate motive for modifying external circumstances 'to good ends'.[52] Something of the two-part theory of morality survived then, but rather less than one would imagine on reading the 1838 essay.

We have now made the differences between Mill's utilitarianism and old-fashioned Benthamism tolerably clear. The new philosophy of movement rested upon a poetic ideal of individual self-development. In that respect, Benthamism was completely bankrupt. Bentham's principle of utility was an adequate philosophical guide for the purposes of legislation, and this was the half truth contained within the old-fashioned system. In legal philosophy an individual's motives could be taken to be either good or bad solely by reference to their effects or consequences: actions, not character, mattered. Mill also saw some merit in Bentham's straightforward view of law as 'practical business'; after all, the absurdities of all technical systems needed to be exposed. But further than this he would not go. While Benthamism deserved praise as a doctrine of legal or legislative reform, it could never serve as an intellectual basis for radicalism. The notion of motivation and the whole idea of human nature was far too narrow and small-minded. The system lacked generosity and tolerance, dealing only with the '*petite-morale*' and with the grubby satisfaction of interests. 'Man is never recognised by him as a being capable of pursuing spiritual perfection as an end': 'one would never imagine from reading him that any human being ever did an act merely because it is right, or abstained from it because it is wrong.'[53] In Mill's view, Bentham had considered interest only 'in the vulgar sense'; that is, as purely self-regarding satisfaction. No consideration had been given to the existence of common purpose or purposes. These were the defining characteristics of social and political collaboration, the source of all that made considered agreement possible. The new radicalism required a philosophy of agreement, not one of conflict. With Benthamism, however, the permanence of competitive and self-regarding desires had to be accepted as a matter of indifference, except when the other-regarding consequences were demonstrably pernicious. Consequently, the old system had offered no incentive for the improvement of individual character and no motives other than fear or hope for responsible social conduct. The instruments of deterrence and sanction were the only means considered. Utilitarianism and social education had been made incompatible, and radicalism had been cut off from its main hope of progress, the moral and mental cultivation of the people. The *Autobiography* stated the new utilitarianism very simply and very clearly. 'I now looked upon the choice of political institutions as a moral and educational question more than one of material interests.'[54]

Mill had resolved the problems of Benthamism to his own satisfaction and had begun to fashion a new variant of utilitarianism by the time the essay on 'Bentham' was published in 1838. His active commitment to the radical party began to diminish after that, though he never returned to his earlier extreme quietism. The new philosophy of movement, in fact, was effectively completed by the publication of the essay on 'Coleridge' in 1840, being reiterated in the savage review of Whewell's moral philosophy published in 1852 in the *Westminster Review*. Mill's later writings dealing with utilitarianism and with the connections between utility and the experiential philosophy are few in number and add little that is dramatically new or different. Obviously, there are marked differences of emphasis, as one would expect: the concerns are not identical, they do not persist unchanged through time. There is, for instance, a far more explicit development of the relationship between justice and utility, emphasising the 'primary moralities' and the rules of conduct common to all stable societies. There is also, possibly, rather more stress on different kinds of pleasure and on the different activities from which pleasure can be derived. Mill's debating speech on Wordsworth had accepted the superiority of some minds and of some pleasures over others; Bentham had also been constantly criticised for his blank indifference to better motives. But the well-known distinction between qualitative and quantitative notions of pleasure, between the satisfaction of Socrates and the satisfaction of the pig, appeared first in Mill's diary for 23 March 1854 and then quite regularly afterwards.[55] The question of proof also was probably much more in Mill's mind as time went on, particularly the question of which faculties were employed in deciding on ultimate ends. The notorious 'proof' of the principle of utility in the *Utilitarianism*, for instance, effectively rested on a psychological argument about the ends which man could be shown to desire— hence, the rather unfortunate analogy Mill made between desiring something and seeing something.

Mill might also have felt that he had gone a little too far in some of his early criticisms of Benthamism. In the *Autobiography* he mentioned that 'there had been excess' in his 'reaction against Benthamism'.[56] But there was never any question of a return to the Benthamite system. This is a contentious point; not all commentators would agree. Some are inclined to present his critique of Benthamism as a romantic and youthful aberration, a summer silliness, overcome with the maturity of the years. Others picture Mill bolting back to Bentham 'when scared by the turnip-ghost of a leviathan-state'.[57] These are exaggerated views, resting on very flimsy evidence. While Mill may have regretted the tone of some of his early criticisms, he never renounced them. On the contrary, he always maintained that they were perfectly fair and eminently just, and even the most casual of observers can detect a great deal of continuity between his early criticisms of old-fashioned Benthamism and his later pronouncements. We need only point to one or two similarities here.

The essays on *Utilitarianism*, for instance, first published as magazine articles in 1861 but completed as papers in the late fifties, maintain all of the decisive points that Mill had developed during his retreat from Benthamism.[58] The moral sense is still presented as natural and organic, a product of man's social nature. This was the 'firm foundation' of utilitarian morality. The feelings of pleasure and pain, of rewards and punishments, were not held to be the sole determinants of conduct. As before, Mill recognised no 'inherent necessity that any human being should be a selfish egotist, devoid of every feeling or care but those which centre in his own miserable individuality'. Again, Mill placed great emphasis on mental and emotional culture, on the ability to pursue virtue for its own sake and on the disinterested growth of concern for others. The earlier eclectic theme of agreement is also present: there were *axiomata media* available to the utilitarian, and Mill restated his belief that many diverse schools could agree about these secondary or intermediate maxims. 'The corollaries from the principle of utility, like the precepts of every practical art, admit of indefinite improvement.' Quite simply, there was no need to test each action by first principles when such 'intermediate generalisations' or corollaries were available. The romantic emphasis on inner character and personal culture also remained strongly imprinted on the argument. While Mill was now less sure about the merits of Goethe, in his diary for 2 March 1854, there is a passage absolutely faithful to the spirit of Wordsworth, Coleridge and Shelley.

> 'It is a common saying that the only true test of a person's character is actions. There is much error in this ... Actions, no doubt, are the fittest test for the world at large, because all they want to know of a man is the actions they may expect from him. But to his intimates, who care about what he is and not merely about what he does, the involuntary indications of feeling and disposition are a much surer criterion of them than voluntary acts.'[59]

The essay 'On Genius', we remind ourselves, had offered the same argument well over twenty years before. The essays on *Utilitarianism* also stated a notion of cultivation very familiar to those who knew of Mill's defence of Wordsworth. The cultivated mind could find excitement and an inexhaustible interest, 'in the objects of nature, the achievements of art, the imaginations of poetry, the incidents of history ...' Next to selfishness, it was 'want of mental cultivation' which 'makes life unsatisfactory'.[60] These are general resemblances, not detailed identities, but Mill's philosophy of utilitarianism had remained a philosophy of individual self-culture, tolerant of variety and firmly opposed to the logic and spirit of Benthamism. On the evidence available, no other conclusion is really plausible: Mill was both a romantic and a utilitarian, and he remained so throughout his life.

Notes Chapter II

1 'Tennyson's Poems', J. B. Schneewind (ed.), *Mill's Essays on Literature and Society* (New York, Collier-Macmillan, 1965), p. 143. This Coleridgean notion of imagination appeared again and again in the early and middle thirties. See, for instance, J. R. Hainds, 'J. S. Mill's Examiner Articles on Art', *Journal of the History of Ideas*, vol. XI, no. 2, 1950, pp. 215–34. On the German background, there is the excellent W. H. Bruford, *The German Tradition of Self-Cultivation* (London, Cambridge Univ. Press, 1975). For a more general account of Mill's own literary theories see M. H. Abrams, *The Mirror and the Lamp: Romantic*

Theory of the Critical Tradition (London, O.U.P., 1953); also Edward Alexander, *Mathew Arnold and John Stuart Mill* (New York, Columbia Univ. Press, 1965).

2 *Essays on Economics and Society* (Toronto, Univ. of Toronto Press, 1967), *Collected Works*, vol. IV, p. 337. Mill continued the argument in true eclectic fashion: 'he must endeavour to place himself at their point of view, and strive earnestly to see the object as they see it'.

3 J. Stillinger (ed.), *Autobiography* (London, O.U.P., 1971), pp. 91–2.

4 ibid., p. 67.

5 'The Two Kinds of Poetry', *Essays on Literature and Society*, op. cit., pp. 120–1.

6 ibid., pp. 128–9.

7 'Tennyson's Poems', op. cit., p. 141.

8 *Autobiography*, op. cit., p. 83.

9 'Professor Sedgwick's Discourse on the Studies of the University of Cambridge', *Essays on Ethics, Religion and Society* (Toronto, Univ. of Toronto Press, 1969), *Collected Works*, vol. X, p. 60. The connections between this argument and some of the passages of the *Analysis of the Phenomena of the Human Mind* have been examined by G. W. Spence in 'The Psychology behind J. S. Mill's Proof', *Philosophy*, Jan. 1968, vol. XLII, no. 163, pp. 18–28.

10 Mill to Nichol, *The Earlier Letters of John Stuart Mill, 1812–1848* (Toronto Univ. of Toronto Press, 1963), *Collected Works*, vol. XIII, p. 738.

11 Mill to Carlyle, *Letters*, op. cit., XII, p. 149.

12 'On Genius', *Essays on Literature and Society*, op. cit., pp. 91–2. Mill published this essay in the *Monthly Repository* in October 1832. Possibly it is his most 'romantic' or 'mystic' essay, written in a rather clumsy style. He said of it himself: 'it was written in the height of my Carlylism, a vice of style which I have since carefully striven to correct'. Mill to Lewes, *Letters*, op. cit., XIII, p. 449.

13 Mill to Carlyle, *Letters*, op. cit., XII, pp. 153 and 163.

14 Mill to d'Eichthal, *Letters*, op. cit., XIII, p. 404.

15 Mill to Sterling, ibid., p. 407.

16 Mill to Fonblanque, ibid., p. 370. Mill continued: 'Have you forgotten, what I am sure you once knew, that my opinion of their philosophy is and has for years been *more* unfavourable by far than your own? And that my radicalism is of a school the most remote from theirs, at all points, which exists?'

17 H. N. Pym, *Memories of Old Friends; being extracts from the Journals and letters of Caroline Fox* (London, Smith & Elder, 1882), 2nd edn, vol. I, p. 216.

18 J. Morley, *Recollections* (London, Macmillan & Co., 1917), vol. I, p. 67.

19 Mill to Nichol, *Letters*, op. cit., XII, p. 221.

20 ibid., p. 207.

21 ibid., p. 312. Mill then wrote: 'My object will now be to draw together a body of writers resembling the old school of radicals only in being on the Movement side, in philosophy, morality, and art as well as in politics and socialities.'

22 Many of the details of this renewed interest in radicalism are given in Joseph Hamburger, *Intellectuals in Politics: John Stuart Mill and the Philosophic Radicals* (New Haven, Yale Univ. Press, 1965). There is also some information in William Thomas, 'The Philosophic Radicals', in P. Hollis (ed.), *Pressure from Without* (London, Edward Arnold, 1974), pp. 52–79.

23 Mill to Carlyle, *Letters*, op. cit., XII, p. 134.

24 ibid, p. 168.

25 *Autobiography*, op. cit., p. 123.

26 'Civilization', *Essays on Literature and Society*, op. cit., pp. 148–82. 'Writings of Junius Redivivus', *Tait's Edinburgh Magazine*, vol. 3, 1833, pp. 347–54. Junius Redivivus was the pseudonym of William Bridges Adams (1797–1872), whose first wife was the daughter of Francis Place; he was a regular contributor to the *Monthly Repository*. See F. E. Mineka, *The Dissidence of Dissent: The Monthly Repository, 1806–1838* (Chapel Hill, Univ. of N. Carolina Press, 1944). Mill held a very high opinion of Adams and recommended him strongly to Carlyle.

27 'Junius Redivivus', op. cit., p. 349.

28 'Reorganization of the Reform Party', *Westminster Review*, April 1839, vol. XXXII, pp. 475–508. This article was ready in January 1838, but the outbreak of the Canadian rebellion held up publication. It is Mill's longest and most considered piece of writing on the aims and organisation of the radical party; it is particularly revealing of his views on the relationship between social class and political attitude.

29 'Junius Redivivus', op. cit., p. 349.

30 ibid., p. 350.

31 'Reorganization of the Reform Party', op. cit., p. 494.

32 ibid., p. 475.

33 Mill to Macvey Napier, *Letters*, op. cit., XIII, p. 430. See also the *Autobiography*, pp. 128–9.

34 'Remarks on Bentham's Philosophy', *Essays on Ethics, Religion and Society* op. cit., p. 13. Though the echo of Wordsworth is very clear, Macaulay's critique of James Mill's theory of government had made the identical point in very similar language: 'There is nothing which may not, by association or by comparison, become an object either of desire or of aversion.' T. Babington Macaulay, 'Mill's Essay on Government', *Essays, Critical and Miscellaneous* (Boston, Phillips, Sampson & Co., 1856), new and revised edition, p. 682.

35 *Autobiography*, op. cit., p. 86.

36 *A System of Logic* (London, Longman, 1970), bk VI, ch. 2, p. 551.

37 *Autobiography*, op. cit., p. 106; and see also pp. 107–8. Mill's relationship with Austin's wife was less happy. She gossiped about Mill and Harriet Taylor and in the early draft of the *Autobiography* she was described as having 'a very mischievous tongue'. Mill was equally severe on members of his own family who spoke about their relationship.

38 Mill to Ward, *The Later Letters of John Stuart Mill, 1849–1873* (Toronto, Univ. of Toronto Press, 1972), *Collected Works*, vol. XV, pp. 649–50.

39 'Sedgwick', op. cit., p. 56.

40 'Bentham', *Essays on Ethics, Religion and Society*, op. cit., p. 98.

41 Mill to Carlyle, *Letters*, op. cit., XII, pp. 207–8.

42 Mill to Robert Barclay Fox, *Letters*, op. cit., XIII, p. 426.

43 'Bentham', op. cit., p. 113.

44 'Remarks on Bentham's Philosophy', op. cit., p. 8.

45 *The Friend* (London, William Pickering, 1837), vol. II, Essay XI, p. 169. Our previous quotation came from *Aids to Reflection* (Liverpool, Edward Howell, 1874), 'On Sensibility', Aphorism XXXVII, p. 41. Mill read a great deal of Coleridge in the late thirties including *The Lay Sermons, Literary Remains, The Friend* and *Aids to Reflection*. He also read *Confessions of an Inquiring Spirit* six years before it was published in a transcript that John Sterling possessed. Very little has been written in detail on Mill's relationship with Coleridge, but there is C. C. R. Turk, *Samuel Taylor Coleridge and John Stuart Mill*, D.Phil. thesis, Univ. of Sussex, 1970. An excellent general study of Coleridge and nineteenth-century liberalism is C. R. Sanders, *Coleridge and the Broad Church Movement* (Durham, N. Carolina Press, 1942).

46 'On Genius', op. cit., p. 88.

47 'Sedgwick', op. cit., p. 56.

48 'Bentham', op. cit., pp. 98–9.

49 ibid., p. 98.

50 ibid., p. 95.

51 ibid., p. 112.

52 'Remarks on Bentham's Philosophy', op. cit., p. 15.

53 'Bentham', op. cit., p. 95.

54 *Autobiography*, op. cit., p. 102.

55 Mill's Diary, Hugh Elliot (ed.), *The Letters of John Stuart Mill* (London, Longmans et al., 1960), vol. II, Appendix A, p. 381. One recalls Carlyle's phrase 'pig-philosophy'.

56 *Autobiography*, op. cit., p. 137. But see also p. 130: 'The substance of this criticism I still think perfectly just; but I have sometimes doubted whether it was right to publish it at that time. I have often felt that Bentham's philosophy, as an instrument of progress, has been to some extent discredited before it had done its work.'

57 Our phrase is from R. J. White, 'John Stuart Mill', *Cambridge Journal*, vol. V, no. 2, 1951, p. 89. The right emphasis seems to be given by F. E. L. Priestley in his scholarly introduction to the *Essays on Ethics, Religion and Society, Collected Works*, vol. X. He recognises a change in Mill's tactics, with rather less emphasis on the deficiencies of Benthamism; at the same time, he points out that while Mill was prepared to defend Bentham, he was never very happy doing so.

58 *Utilitarianism*, reprinted in *Essays on Ethics, Religion and Society*, op. cit.; see in particular pp. 211–12, 215–16, 220–1 and 224–5. *Utilitarianism* was obviously a popular and rather casual exposition. In fact, Mill was hardly bothered about detailed corrections and long explanations. When Theodor Gomperz pointed out the equivocation involved in the use of the words 'desired' and 'desirable', Mill simply authorised him to remove the whole passage from the German translation. On this point, see Adelaide Weinberg,

Theodor Gomperz and John Stuart Mill (Geneva, Librairie Droz, 1963), p. 51–3. This attitude is also reflected in the *Autobiography*. Mill makes hardly any mention of the essays in comparison with his treatment of the *Logic*, the *Principles* and *On Liberty*.

59 Mill's Diary, op. cit., p. 376.

60 *Utilitarianism*, p. 216.

Chapter III

Science and the Authority of the Instructed

Although commitment to the radical party and the elaboration of an ethic of self-development marked the end of Mill's quietism, re-awakening an active interest in politics and in party causes which was to persist throughout his life, they did not seriously alter his view of the purpose of political philosophy. This had been firmly fixed by his eclecticism. Mill stayed on the track of compromise. Narrow and proselytising commitments were to be avoided; agreement remained the prime object, and agreement could only be made generous and tolerant by avoiding sectarianism, by promoting disinterested and virtuous ideals and by the sparing use of first principles. Without this spirit of sympathetic tolerance, self-culture would be impossible; the national character would be confirmed in its habits and radicalism would continue to be a narrow and merely sectional creed, making no appeal in the country at large or in the colonies overseas. But while he was convinced of the need for individual self-culture, and while the radical party would work for educational and social reforms, Mill also believed that ignorance would inevitably remain. In that respect, his open-hearted pragmatism was combined with a kind of pessimism. Knowledge, like experience, was very difficult to acquire; time, leisure and a certain sensibility were needed, and not all classes had the same opportunity of enjoying these. Like John Austin, Mill inclined to the view that the mass or multitude was not in a position to acquire a clear understanding of the appropriate criteria for public conduct.[1] The many were debarred from just that kind of knowledge which made rational and disinterested conduct possible.

Also, as we have already seen, Mill's work for the radical party tended to confirm this view, at least by implication. The philosophy of movement did not suppose a sudden or significant transformation of human nature. Radicalism was not populism. The aristocratic principle of excellence remained important. Superior knowledge or insight still demanded respect, and the true radical was bound to recognise the complexities of government, fully accepting the need for special and unusual skills. The majority did not possess these skills; they were also unlikely to acquire them. In Mill's view this raised many problems, particularly given a tendency for the masses to predominate more and more in politics. He was not fatalistic, however: ignorance did not make good government impossible; while it was a hindrance, it was far from being decisive. With popular and representative institutions, the few could still be made responsible to the many without the many actually governing. Mill was always emphatic on this point. There was no need for 'the many themselves to be perfectly wise; it is sufficient, if they be duly sensible of the value of superior wisdom'.[2] In fact, pessimism about the capacities of the multitude was more than balanced by confidence in the deferential character of the English: the many would continue to follow the few, trusting their judgement and accepting their reasoning. Consequently, ignorance would remain politically unimportant while deference was sure to continue: 'for the experience of ages, and especially of all great national emergencies, bears out the assertion, that whenever the multitude are really alive to the necessity of superior intellect, they rarely fail to distinguish those who possess it'.[3] The sources of this confidence are easy to locate. Even with the advent of democracy and with a far greater degree of self-culture, Mill believed the English would continue to respect superior knowledge and so remain deferential. The habit of obedience would continue, and there would be none of the *incivisme* common in other European countries. The arrival of the mass in politics would not mean the departure of intellectual authority. The élite would remain because the English would stay sensible and reliable, even if a little mundane. These views, of course, were the foundation for the essay on *Representative Government*, an essay arguing strongly for government by professionals and experts.

At this time, however, in the early and middle thirties, Mill was very prone to emphasise agreement amongst the instructed few themselves. No precise date can be given for this view. But more and more after the crisis, Mill related the political authority of a group to that group's consensus on doctrine and method. Deference was a product of this rather than of anything else. Only in times of rapid transition was such a consensus likely to be absent, or to be present only intermittently. This view may well have been borrowed directly from the Saint-Simonian thinkers; the *Autobiography* certainly suggests this was the case. Like the Saint-Simonians, Mill believed every society to be in a 'natural' and balanced state when two conditions were fulfilled: first, when the social foundations were not in constant question; secondly, when the instructed few were broadly agreed in their thinking. Like the Saint-Simonians, Mill had concluded that the mass or multitude would not defer with confidence if there was division and dissent amongst the instructed classes themselves. Usually, this conclusion was asserted at a high level of generality as part of Mill's reflections on the nature of science. But Mill was increasingly inclined to use the argument from consensus in interpreting political history. In his first review of Tocqueville's writings, for instance, Mill expressed a belief that American politics were considerably weakened by the lack of a highly instructed class capable of inspiring reverence;[4] the Americans lacked the qualities of deference for this very reason.

These kinds of observation have to be treated carefully: they do not always form part of a serious and coherent explanatory system. But the Saint-Simonian idea of consensus, which presumed a distinction between organic and critical periods, between natural and merely transitional ages, was crucial to Mill's notion of science and to his understanding of the relationship between science and political authority. Agreement was an organic and natural condition, and increasingly Mill was led to the idea that the physical sciences were ideal or paradigm sciences precisely because they guaranteed agreement. They were paradigmatic in other respects as well: they offered complete examples of induction. The law of the composition of forces in dynamics, for instance, 'was the most complete example of the logical process I was investigating'; in applying the law, the mind was only performing 'a simple act of addition'.[5] Physical scientists were also able to derive a great deal from a few general propositions. They worked with the highest and best kind of science, Mill thought, that which used a few well-tested laws to reach a great many valid inferences. But the paradigmatic nature of the physical sciences was mainly due to there being no liberty of conscience amongst the instructed. In these sciences, conclusions could be given a full-hearted and unanimous support. Just as there was no inalienable right of disagreement, so there were no grounds in physical science for taking each person's opinion to be as sound as every other. This was an attractive prospect for an eclectic of Mill's kind. Agreement was not only pragmatically justified, it was also scientifically proper, and Mill explained to d'Eichthal just what his hopes were in this respect. The physical sciences were an example of 'the ultimate end towards which we are advancing and which we shall one day attain, a state in which the body of the people, i.e. the uninstructed, shall entertain the same feelings of deference and submission to the authority of the instructed, in morals and politics, as they at present do in the physical sciences'.[6] In the *Autobiography* Mill admitted, appropriately enough, that he had learnt this 'lesson' from 'the early work of Comte'. The writings of

Herschel might also have brought the lesson home. The physical sciences were certain to be minority sciences because they presumed 'a degree of knowledge of mathematics and geometry altogether unattainable by the generality of mankind'.[7] Those with knowledge of physical science were unlikely to be challenged by the mass. Authority would not only be certain, it would also be safe.

This belief in certain and safe authority, so reminiscent of Mill's early toryism, is central to the *Logic* itself, although commentators occasionally fail to point it out. Once the study of man and society was lifted from a condition of unresolved and rather puzzled speculation to a condition analogous to the physical sciences, unanimity became a real possibility. The truths of politics would then resemble the truths of astronomy, being accepted in the same way, with the same beneficial consequences for political practice. For this reason, possibly, Mill was very concerned when he wrote the *Logic* to avoid provoking philosophical controversy. While the book could hardly be described as neutral, Mill himself hoped that it would offend no one. He stressed in his introduction that the work had 'no necessary connexion with any particular views respecting the ulterior analysis': logic was the 'common ground on which the partisans of Hartley and of Reid, of Locke and of Kant may meet and join hands'.[8] In fact, the *Logic* can easily be interpreted as part of a continuing eclectic enterprise to encourage agreement and to bring together diverse schools of philosophic thought. Mill's romanticism had not led him to exclude science; on the contrary, science was one possible basis for the agreement all eclectics welcomed. Mill himself was very quick to recognise the implications of such an ambition. If science was an institution with social and political consequences, then the 'decay of old opinions, and the agitation that disturbs European society to its inmost depths' made the question whether 'moral and social phenomena are really exceptions to the general certainty and uniformity of the course of nature', a question of immediate political relevance.[9] The connections Mill saw between science, unanimity and stable political authority are the main concern of this chapter. Two general questions are unavoidable: whether Mill really believed in an absolute unanimity of opinion amongst the instructed, and whether he thought a physical or positive science of politics either possible or desirable. A good deal turns on the answers to these questions. Some commentators take consensus to be Mill's basic value: a consensus founded upon a science of politics strictly analogous to the physical sciences. From here, it is only a short step to the 'authoritarian' Mill; to the Mill concerned solely with the individuality of the elevated and instructed and with their protection from the mundane mediocrity of mass opinion.

One should acknowledge straight away that the paradigmatic character of the physical sciences had no value for Mill unless there was agreement amongst the practitioners themselves. Where private judgement was so exercised that either no agreement existed at all, or existed only sparsely and intermittently, then the uninstructed would be less likely to defer to the authority of the few. One security for good government would be endangered, the many would fall back on their ignorance and special knowledge would become either less important generally or less relevant to decision making. For Mill this was a frightening prospect. The early draft of his *Autobiography* shows the extent of his fear and his hopes for a solution. Whilst insisting he had not become 'one atom less zealous for increasing the knowledge and improving the understanding of the many', he also admitted 'my hopes of improvement rested less on the reason of the multitude than on the possibility of effecting such an improvement in the methods of political and social philosophy, as should enable all thinking and instructed persons . . . to be so nearly of one mind on these subjects, as to carry the multitude with them by their united authority'.[10] Stable politics required unanimity amongst the intellectual élite; there can be no doubt at all that Mill eased his worries about the apparent inevitability of democracy by reminding himself of this agreement amongst 'all thinking and instructed persons'.

In short, Mill counted very much on consensus. The English habit of obedience would only continue if the educated few were agreed amongst themselves; this was essential in assisting the many to defer and in maintaining political stability. Democracy would be safely sheltered by a clear intellectual authority—a point which Mill was very fond of illustrating from the politics of his own day. In his first review of Tocqueville, for example, he chose the issue of free trade. According to Mill, this showed that 'on those points on which the instructed classes are agreed', the uninstructed would be quick to adopt their opinions. Methodological agreement made the best kind of political sense; when such agreement existed, 'we have no fear but that the many will not only defer to their authority, but cheerfully acknowledge them as their superiors in wisdom, and the fittest to rule'. Agreement was the crucial fact: doubt and dispute would be fatal. 'The multitude will never believe these truths, until tendered to them from an authority in which they have as unlimited confidence as they have in the unanimous voice of astronomers on a question of astronomy.'[11] Our first question seems to have been answered. Agreement was not merely desirable, it was politically indispensable.

The analogy between the physical sciences and the study of morals and politics was an awkward one, however, and this awkwardness has

73

to be brought out in order to maintain the proper perspective. While Mill accepted the paradigmatic nature of the physical sciences, he obviously had serious epistemological doubts about a strictly positivist account of knowledge: all his writings after the crisis show that. He had also rejected the idea of a permanent human nature subject to exact and invariant laws: this was the Benthamite fallacy exposed by the Saint-Simonians. Human nature was not the same at all times and in all places. While Mill's revised or corrected utilitarianism did not rule out the search for a systematic knowledge of human nature, particularly of man's social nature, it did imply a sharp distinction between truths and rules; between the propositions of science and the precepts of art. If morals and politics were to be considered as practical arts, then they were of necessity to be characterised by the proposing of many different ends. The rules or precepts which were appropriate to them were not a matter of science at all; they were irremediably provisional and imperfect, being tied in to the contingencies of time, place and circumstance. Moreover, the proposing of ends, which was the defining characteristic of art, presupposed liberty of conscience and the right to make and to promulgate one's own judgement of right and wrong. Self-culture completely ruled out the imposition of rules of conduct, or of standards of behaviour, on the authority of superior knowledge. All true knowledge came from within. No one could have his ideas made for him, and for agreement to exist at all, there had to be continuous free inquiry. The right of private judgement was not, then, merely nominal as it was in mathematics and physics; this was true whether the many were ignorant or not. In all of these respects, the analogy with the physical sciences was not only very awkward, but also severely limited.

Mill would seem to have recognised these limitations early on. There is certainly a lot of textual evidence to this effect, which we cannot ignore as many commentators do. In one of his earliest statements of the idea that 'moral and social science' might become as perfect as the physical sciences, Mill pointed to all of the conditions that would have to be fulfilled. The theory and practice of education would have to be greatly improved. People would also need to acquire new conceptions of themselves; they would have to learn how 'to cultivate and nurture their own susceptibilities of happiness, and have made such arrangements of outward circumstances, as shall provide that the means which each adopts of seeking his own well-being, shall no longer damage that of the remainder of his species'.[12] This is hardly the language of scientism. Even those articles published as 'The Spirit of the Age', which were written at a high point of Saint-Simonian influence, were careful to stress the right of private judgement and to point to the need for free inquiry. Mill was once asked how social science could be taught to the uneducated and whether the physical sciences were the most important aspect of such an education; his reply is very revealing. 'What the poor as well as the rich require is not to be indoctrinated, is not to be taught other people's opinions, but to be induced and enabled to think for themselves. It is not physical science that will do this, even if they could learn it much more thoroughly than they are able to do.' The answer was wide reading: this would enable them to become 'cultivated beings, which they would not become by following out, even to the greatest length, physical science'. In fact, these sciences were not all that important. 'Free discussion with them as equals, in speech and in writing', Mill concluded, 'seems the best instruction that can be given them, specially on social subjects.'[13] Respect for the authority of the physical scientist hardly seems to be present here.

One other general point should be made. Mill had elaborated his variant of utilitarianism with the romantic antithesis between reason and feeling very much in mind. As we have seen, he shared a good deal of Wordsworth's and Coleridge's strong antipathy to enlightenment rationalism, and while he never abandoned the habit of close and precise analysis, Mill could not take the scientific disposition to be simply a rational calculus of discovery in which imaginative insight was irrelevant and misleading. The physical sciences were necessary, but they were not sufficient. Systematic knowledge required a union of philosophy and poetry, and emotion and feeling were just as significant as analysis. Mill's diary for 11 March 1854 stated his position succinctly:

'Thought and feeling in their lower degrees antagonize, in their higher harmonize. Much thought and little feeling make a mental voluptuary who wastes life in intellectual exercise for its own sake. Much feeling and little thought are the common material of a bigot and fanatic. Much feeling and much thought make the hero or heroine.'[14]

One would be silly to make too much of an entry in a diary. But Mill's commitment to a union of thought and feeling was bound to suggest that the precepts of morals and politics were many and varied, resembling a loose body of sensitive suggestions rather than a system of universal truths that admitted of no variation or exception. This was certainly the view taken in Mill's correspondence with John Austin. The study of politics could not be freed from the limitations inherent in particular situations. Politics was inevitably a pragmatic, piecemeal and untidy business, and in considering the 'province of government', for instance, there were no *axiomata media* 'which do not vary with time, place and circumstance. I doubt if much more can be done in a scientific treatment of the question than to point out a certain number of pros and a certain number of cons of a more or less general application, and with some attempt at an estimation of the comparative importance of each, leaving the balance to be struck in each particular case as it arises'.[15] Mill could hardly have been more pragmatic than this. It was precisely this kind of cautious and piecemeal attitude to science and to problem solving which balanced Mill's admiration for the authoritative and universal statements possible in the physical sciences. In fact, he held to the analogy between the physical sciences and morals and politics only in a highly qualified and tentative fashion. And while the prospect of agreement was very appealing, Mill's absolute insistence upon each person thinking for himself and refusing to take ideas on trust from the authority of others, was bound to sustain his doubts about the paradigmatic character of the physical sciences. These doubts, in turn, were sharpened by Mill's willingness to accept a clear distinction between art and science.

The distinction between art and science appears again and again in Mill's writings. It was first stated systematically, however, in 'On the Definition of Political Economy', an essay written in the autumn of 1831 and partly rewritten in the summer of 1833. Although this essay formed the basis for Mill's treatment of the relation between art and science in the final book of the *Logic*, it was published after the *Logic* in 1844. Mill began by noting, as Coleridge had done, that practice precedes theory. The definition of a science invariably follows the creation of that science; 'like the wall of a city, it has usually been erected, not to be a receptacle for such edifices as might afterwards spring up, but to circumscribe an aggregation already in existence'. In common with many other sciences, political economy lacked an adequate definition. The popular and vulgar notion of the subject, 'that Political Economy is a science which teaches, or professes to teach, in what manner a nation may be made rich', was open to a 'conclusive objection'. Mill stated the objection at some length. This definition of political economy

'confounds the essentially distinct, though closely connected, ideas of *science* and *art*. These two ideas differ from one another as the understanding differs from the will, or as the indicative mood in grammar differs from the imperative. The one deals in facts, the other in precepts. Science is a collection of *truths*; art, a body of *rules*, or directions for conduct. The language of science is, This is, or, This is not; This does, or does not happen. The language of art is, Do this; Avoid that. Science takes cognizance of a *phenomenon* and endeavours to discover its *law*; art proposes to itself an *end*, and looks out for means to effect it'.[16]

Mill elaborated this distinction in various ways in the essay, but he gave one 'of the strongest reasons for drawing the line of separation clearly and broadly between science and art' in a footnote to his argument. The principle of classification in science 'most conveniently follows the classification of causes, while arts must necessarily be classified according to the classification of the effects, the production of which is their appropriate end'.

Several conclusions might legitimately be drawn from this distinction. Mill would seem to have avoided the naturalistic fallacy; 'is' statements and 'ought' statements are clearly distinguished; the difference between the understanding and the will could well refer back to Coleridge again, confirming the impact of romantic epistemology. One conclusion is of immediate relevance, however. If morals and politics were taken to be arts rather than sciences, then there could be no question of proving the principles upon which they rested. The language of art was the language of ends, and this language, being concerned with value judgements, was a species of imperative which could not be shown to be either true or false. Strictly speaking, the language of art made no verifiable statements at all; as a language or mode of exposition, it simply enunciated ends or values which the practitioner found desirable and appropriate. At the time Mill made this distinction, in the early part of the thirties, he also distinguished between morals and politics, arguing that while there was both an art and a science of politics, politics being concerned with truths and rules, with 'phenomena' as well as 'ends', this was not the case with ethics or morality. 'Morality itself is not a science, but an art; not truths, but rules.'[17] Mill also admitted, however, that the rules of art presupposed the truths of science. It is clear what he meant: once an end had been enunciated, then the question of means to this end, which was not a question of validity but only of ways of arriving at a given outcome, was a matter for science. The question was analogous with any matter of fact and required only the indicative mood. In this case, while art and science were connected and while 'the reasons of a maxim of policy, or of any other rule of art, can be no other than the theorems of the corresponding science', art and science still remained distinct. To define a subject as 'art' was necessarily to suppose 'one first principle, or general major premise, not borrowed from science; that which enunciates the object aimed at, and affirms it to be a desirable object'.[18] And although the ultimate standard for assessing such objects was the principle of utility, the principle itself was not susceptible of proof. As is well known, Mill believed that it was impossible to prove the truth of statements about ultimate or final ends; they were simply beyond the scope of science.

In general, of course, Mill's notion of science and scientific explanation was true to the deductive approach of Locke and Newton. The *Logic* itself was intended as a reply to the commonsense experimentalism of Bacon, particularly as taken up and used by Macaulay and the Whig empiricists. We also know that Mill always condemned 'empiricism'. In his earliest writings on science in the *Examiner*, Mill praised Herschel for demonstrating 'the superiority of science over empiricism under the name of *common sense*—of the advantage of *systematic* investigation, and high general cultivation of the intellect'.[19] It is quite clear what Mill understood by 'systematic' in this context. 'Whatever be the phenomenon which is the subject of inquiry, we discover the *law* of that phenomenon, by ascertaining what are the circumstances which are invariably found to be present whenever it occurs.' In other words, scientists should always attempt to reach laws which are ultimate or unconditional. Mill was adamant that 'it is only in art, as distinguished from science, that we can with propriety speak of exceptions'.[20] Consequently, on Mill's view, an individual occurrence or event was explained by the production of a law-like general statement and by a statement of initial conditions. This 'hypothetico-deductive' conception of science is very familiar. Popper characterised the whole conception in *The Logic of Scientific Discovery*. 'To give a *causal explanation* of an event means to deduce a statement which describes it, using as premisses of the deduction one or more *universal laws*, together with certain singular statements, the *initial conditions*.'[21] Mill's own attempt to define the meaning of explanation in science was essentially similar to this. To explain an occurrence or event in terms of its cause was necessarily to make reference to a universal law: the aim of the scientist being to explain as many phenomena as possible from as few such laws as possible; systematic explanation always involving the most general of hypotheses.

The *Logic* exemplifies this approach very well. As Mill explained, the 'whole problem of the investigation of nature' was comprehended in one question: 'What are the fewest assumptions, which being granted, the order of nature as it exists would be the result.'[22] The greater the generality of the law, Mill argued, the less chance there was of that law 'being ultimately found not to be universally true'. Even so, Mill did specifically reject the idea that any such law or laws would enable the scientist to resolve unfamiliar occurrences or events into familiar ones. Science constantly generated puzzles and the discovery of a law or laws did not necessarily facilitate a move from the unknown to the known. This was not essential to systematic, scientific explanation, even though it was the meaning of explanation in 'common parlance'. On the contrary, 'the process with which we are here concerned', 'resolves a phenomenon with which we are familiar into one of which we previously knew little or nothing'. The logic of scientific discovery, then, was not to point out 'some more familiar, but merely some more general phenomenon, of which it is a partial exemplification'.[23] A similar argument prompted Mill's defence of negative dialectics when reviewing Grote's *History of Greece* in the *Edinburgh Review*. It was the fashion to decry negative dialectics; 'as if making men conscious of their ignorance were not the first step—and an absolutely necessary one—towards inducing them to acquire knowledge'. Mill went on to give some familiar examples of his meaning. Socrates had convinced men of their ignorance; doing this, made positive knowledge possible. Mill even treated Bacon kindly: his war upon confused general ideas, *notiones temere a rebus abstractas*, was essentially negative, 'but it constituted the epoch from which alone advancement in positive knowledge became possible. It is to Bacon that we owe Newton, and the modern physical science'.[24]

We should not give the impression, however, that Mill's notion of science and of scientific explanation was confined to formal deductive inference. That would plainly be false. Obviously, science involved far more than consistency, and reasoning could not be limited to deductive inference from general propositions. Science was also concerned with the truth of premises. Consequently, the logic of consistency needed to be supplemented by a logic of truth; a logic, that is, of observation and experience. This seems to explain why Mill was so attracted to Tocqueville's works. The value of his work on democracy, for instance, was 'less in the conclusions, than in the mode of arriving at them'. 'His method is, as that of a philosopher on such a subject must be—a combination of deduction with induction: his evidences are laws of human nature, on the one hand; the example of America and France, and other modern nations, on the other.'[25] In Mill's view, this was 'the true Baconian and Newtonian method applied to society and government'. Indeed, one compelling reason for writing and for publishing the *Logic* was to expose the poverty of the view that the human mind could arrive at a true knowledge of the world without observation and experience: this was the sort of metaphysical nonsense which made science impossible and made it very difficult for Mill to maintain the eclectic neutrality of the *Logic*; there were no necessary truths knowable by direct intuition of the mind, despite the pretensions of the *a priori* school. Mill explained just where the *Logic* stood on this issue in a letter to Sterling in 1839; 'mine professes to be a logic of *experience* only, and to throw no further light upon the existence of truths not experimental, than is thrown by shewing to what extent reasoning from experience will carry us. Above all mine is a logic of the indicative mood alone—-the logic of the imperative, in which the major premiss says not *is* but *ought*—I do not meddle with'.[26] And it is clear that Mill did take the

Logic to be a permanent refutation of 'the great original error of thinking that an opinion deeply seated in the human mind proves itself'. There were few allies: 'except in the logic, I know not where any real battle is kept up against this *fons errorum*. Every fresh edition is a renewal of the controversy'.[27]

Rightly or wrongly, Mill located the strength of intuitionism in 'morals, politics and religion' 'in the appeal which it is accustomed to make to the evidence of mathematics and of the cognate branches of physical science'.[28] In short, he took the crucial part of the 'supersensual philosophy' to be the identity of truth and self-evidence. To attack here, was to go right to the heart of unprogressive conservative argument, which made opinions their own justification. This view almost certainly reflected Mill's reading of Whewell's *History of the Inductive Sciences*. The Master of Trinity College, Cambridge, had published his work in 1837 and it had served as a great stimulus to complete the writing of the *Logic*. The difference between necessary truths and truths of experience, between universal and merely contingent truths, Whewell had maintained, was that 'necessary truths are those of which we cannot distinctly conceive the contrary'.[29] Geometry and mathematics were the obvious subjects to use in attempting to establish this view. For this reason, Mill was very concerned to show that truth in mathematics and in geometry could be accounted for in inductive terms, that the truths of geometry and mathematics were not special kinds of truths. The second book of the *Logic*, which contained the fiercest part of Mill's attack upon intuitionism, was written to establish precisely this. Mill subjected each part of Whewell's argument to minute scrutiny. The main direction of his attack is well known: axioms were generalisations from observation; they were experimental truths and generalisations could only be known to be true by establishing causal connections between occurrences or events. Consequently, in science, hypotheses aimed at being true in just the same sense as laws of nature were true; the proof of both the hypothesis and the law consisted in particular sequences observed, or in particular sequences correctly predicted. In Mill's view, then, the act of hypothesis was strictly analogous with finding out true statements about the world. The truth of these statements, like the truth of any statement, could only be established by inference from particular fact to particular fact. Consequently, the proof of any single causal law had to be by observation of particulars in conformity to that law; it could never be by deduction from supposed 'laws' of universal causation. Induction was the only valid method of inference to truth, and induction remained very firmly a matter of observation, experience and experiment.

In part, no doubt, the appeal of the physical sciences as paradigms was sustained by this kind of belief in the uniformity and universality of scientific procedures. The physical sciences aimed at producing general laws established by induction: social science should do the same. But the paradigm was that exemplified in mechanics and physics. There were blatant inadequacies in chemistry and geometry. In the *Logic*, of course, Mill explicitly rejected the 'Experimental or Chemical mode of investigation, and the Abstract or Geometrical mode'; both of these were 'radical misconceptions of the proper mode of philosophising on society and government'.[30] Mill's reasons were plain enough. Considering first his objections to chemistry, the argument is simple. Man does not change in society, he is still a man, having no characteristics or properties 'but those which are derived from, and may be resolved into, the laws of the nature of individual man. In social phenomena, the Composition of Causes is the universal law'. This assumption, familiar to us now as the assumption of methodological individualism, made chemistry totally inappropriate. In chemistry, the 'Composition of Causes' was not operative, since chemical phenomena, unlike social phenomena, were subject to changes in kind; indeed, phenomena were radically altered. 'Not a trace of the properties of hydrogen or of oxygen is observable in those of their compound water.'[31] Consequently, in chemistry, the effect of causes was not simply the sum or total 'of the effects which the same causes produce when separate'; the connections of cause and effect in chemistry could only be discovered by special experiment. In Mill's view, there was no place for controlled experiment when one engaged in the study of social phenomena. Although there were many logical objections to the notion of experiments, these were much less serious than the practical limitations; 'we palpably never have the power of trying any. We can only watch those which nature produces, or which are produced for other reasons'.[32] If concrete and specific experiments were impossible, then the methods of experimental inquiry would never produce scientific knowledge of social phenomena.

Mill's objections to the 'Geometrical or Abstract Method' are much more familiar. They confirm all his doubts about sectarian Benthamism, following the critique of rationalism initiated by his mental crisis. In the *Logic* 'the interest-philosophy of the Bentham school' was used as 'the most remarkable example afforded by our own times of the geometrical method in politics'.[33] Mill was thus able to repeat objections which had been arrived at and stated before the *Logic* was published. As before, the eclectic stance was decisive. The 'Geometrical Method' lacked a catholic and comprehensive outlook, being far too narrow and one-sided in its concerns. Although the geometrical school had made 'innumerable allowances' in applying its principles, Mill felt this was still futile. 'There is little chance of making due amends in the super-structure of a theory for the want of sufficient breadth in its foundations. It is unphilosophical to construct a science out of a few of the agencies by which the phenomena are determined.'[34] Here Mill was simply repeating warnings he had already delivered in the essay 'On the Definition of Political Economy' and in his debating speech on Wordsworth. The constant danger was narrowness, the danger of overlooking something. Mere mental discipline was an inadequate protection: the only real safeguard was to understand the views of others, striving 'earnestly to see the object as they see it'. The crucial faculty was imagination, not reason. Mill also repeated his objections to the proposition that men are always motivated by self-interest. This was not true. 'Human beings are not governed in all their actions by their worldly interests.' But even granting the truth of the proposition, like Macaulay Mill believed it could only be true tautologically, amount-ing to the 'identical proposition' that actions were determined by wishes. Mill had many other objections to the 'Geometrical Method'. It was inappropriate since it afforded 'no room for what so constantly occurs in mechanics and in its applications, the case of conflicting forces; of causes which counteract or modify one another'. Overall, however, the defects of the 'Geometrical Method' were identical with the defects of Benthamism; too many conclusions deduced from too few simple premises. 'The phenomena of society do not depend, in essentials, on some one agency or law of human nature, with only inconsiderable modifications from others.'[35]

This persistent eclectic concern to avoid narrowness and partiality, not only led Mill to reject the 'Geometrical Method', it also made a decisive contribution to his understanding of history. The historio-graphy of the enlightenment had been excessively parochial. The English, in particular, read their own history backwards, being very prone to interpret the past as if it were either identical with or essentially similar to the present. For Mill, the study of history was indispensable because it enlarged experience, not because it proved the superiority of any present culture or institution. History was synonymous with variety; historical knowledge was knowledge of diversity and difference. Above all, perhaps, the historian needed sympathy for times and circumstances different from his own. He should have 'some of the characteristics of the poet', able to 'body forth the forms of things unknown'.[36] It was precisely this imaginative reconstruction of other times which made the historian conscious of his own ignorance and more likely to seek a truly comprehensive knowledge; the good historian was constantly aware of the limits of his own language and suppositions. Moreover history was not only a 'record of all great things which have been achieved by mankind', it also gave 'a certain largeness of conception to the student, and familiarises him with the action of great causes'. In Mill's view, no other subject could do this quite so well. History was essential to the eclectic disposition. 'Nowhere else will the infinite varieties of human nature be so vividly brought home to him and anything cramped or one-sided in his own standard of it so effectually corrected.'[37] This was also the view Mill took in his discussion of art and science in the essay 'On the Definition of Political Economy'. After surveying the nature and limits of the *a priori* and the *a posteriori* methods, Mill concluded that 'knowledge of what is called history' is 'useful only in the third degree'. By itself, history proved 'little or nothing':

> 'but the study of it is a corrective to the narrow and exclusive views which are apt to be engendered by observation on a more limited scale. Those who never look backwards, seldom look far forwards: their notions of human affairs, and of human nature itself, are circumscribed within the conditions of their own country and their own times'.[38]

In the *Logic*, of course, Mill extended this argument considerably, particularly in his treatment of the 'Inverse Deductive Method'. History was an essential part of social science because it established uniformities of co-existence and succession among social phenomena. History also enabled the social scientist to understand the requisites for particular kinds of politics and to generalise these requisites into laws. Mill referred back to Coleridge's account of the three necessary conditions for a stable political order, for instance, using the typology of social statics and social dynamics he had borrowed from Comte. Social statics examined the relationship between government and political culture; between 'the form of government existing in any society and the contemporaneous state of civilization'. By analysis of different states of society and then by use of comparison, 'without regard to the order of their succession', it was possible to generate laws of social statics. Although these laws were empirical rather than causal, although social statics was subordinate to social dynamics, some of these laws at least 'are found to follow with so much probability from general laws of human nature, that the consilience of the two processes raises the evidence to proof, and the generalizations to the rank of scientific truths'.[39] Had the negative, analytic philosophers of the eighteenth century known more history, had they 'known human nature under any other type than that of their own age, and of the particular classes of society among whom they lived', like Coleridge, they would have truly understood the necessary conditions for 'habitual submission to law and government'.[40] Although Mill queried too ready a disposition to generalise, pointing to the ease with which wrong generalisations were made from history, nevertheless he took such requisites or conditions to be matters of science. The conditions for political stability could be identified and then subjected to generalisation with something approaching scientific certainty. Whatever the practical difficulties, there was nothing wrong with the enterprise in principle.

For this reason, perhaps, there are times, in the *Logic* in particular, when Mill seems to have adopted a rigorously positivist outlook. Although he was never an uncritical devotee of Comte, he does suggest that the activity of political philosophy and of all abstract political speculation could be replaced by the comparative and empirical investigation of uniform phenomena. Possibly this suggestion was prompted by a desire for common agreement, but it can also be seen to follow from Mill's understanding of science and from his notion of causality. Once the empirical laws which historical study provides have been connected with the laws of human nature, and once the laws determining the co-existence of phenomena have been considered in conjunction with those which determine the succession of phenomena, then science would be complete. Knowledge would be positive rather than metaphysical and largely final in character: 'no important branch of human affairs will be any longer abandoned to empiricism and unscientific surmise; the circle of human knowledge will be complete, and it can only thereafter receive further enlargement by perpetual expansion from within'.[41] Moreover, given an adequate social statics, all prescriptive or normative questions about ideal forms of government, for instance, or about the values politics should encourage, could be reduced quite properly to questions of historical possibility. And all such questions, in principle at least, were answerable by the generation of empirical laws. This 'stamps the endless discussions and innumerable theories respecting forms of government in the abstract as fruitless and worthless for any other purpose than as a preparatory treatment of materials to be afterwards used for the construction of a better philosophy'.[42] This positivist aspiration, with all the implications of a universal and value-free science, runs right through the *Logic*, raising the question of the sense or senses in which Mill thought it proper to speak of a science of politics. If abstract political speculation could be superseded by a body of certain and scientific knowledge analogous with knowledge in the physical sciences, then the status of politics as science is finally settled. The question, presumably, is whether Mill believed this or not. There are several equally plausible answers to the question, all of which can be supported by an examination of Mill's writings.

One answer is simply to deny that politics is a subject for science at all, if science implies the thesis of determinism and the power to predict across a great range of cases. This was the answer given in Mill's *Inaugural Address* as the Lord Rector of the University of St Andrews. Nothing had been said about ethics and politics in the outline of 'a complete scientific education', Mill explained, because these were not the subject of a science 'generally admitted and accepted'.

'Politics cannot be learned once for all, from a text-book, or the instructions of a master. What we require to be taught on that subject, is to be our own teachers. It is a subject on which we have no masters to follow; each must explore for himself, and exercise an independent judgement. Scientific politics do not consist in having a set of con- clusions ready-made, to be applied everywhere indiscriminately, but in setting the mind to work in a scientific spirit to discover in each instance the truths applicable to the given case.'[43]

Whatever particular ambiguities this passage contains, the general drift of argument confirms Mill's pragmatism and the awkwardness of the analogy between the physical and social sciences. In politics, the right of private judgement was very far from being merely nominal. The characteristic of all the practical arts, the proposing of ends, actually presupposed liberty of conscience and the right to make and to promul- gate one's own judgements. But there was no universal method of problem solving; one's inductions could never be complete, and judgement in science, like judgement in other things, could never be entirely freed from the limitations inherent in particular situations. Indeed, Mill's considered view in the *Inaugural Address* and elsewhere was that, in politics, science could only proceed case by case, issue by issue. What mattered was attitude of mind rather than formal method- ology. The scientific attitude differed from other attitudes by its concern for truth and falsity. 'Nearly everything that has ever been ascertained by scientific observers, was brought to light in the attempt to test and verify some theory.'[44] It was this aspect of verification that Mill had been primarily concerned to defend in the *Logic*. Intuitionism was the enemy because prejudices were left unexamined, which in politics was fatal to both liberty and progress. Politics should become a science at least in the sense of endeavouring to embody verification by observation and experience. In one sense, Mill was attempting to establish no more than that.

Another answer, this time with a rather different emphasis, was given in the highly polemical *An Examination of Sir William Hamilton's Philosophy*. As part of an attack on intuitionist metaphysics, Mill distinguished theoretical from practical knowledge; affirmations and reasoning on the one hand from precepts and expertise on the other. In his view, Whately had been absolutely right to see the difference between art and science as largely the difference between practical and theoretical knowledge; this was precisely 'why systems of precepts require to be distinguished from systems of truths'. An 'entirely different classification is required for the purposes of theoretical knowledge, and for those of its practical application'. Not very helpfully for the purposes of exegesis, Mill went on to assert that this was a 'natural and logical' distinction, according 'better with the ends and even with the custom of language' than any other.[45] Possibly he had in mind his earlier distinction between modes of classification. In science classification was of causes whereas in art classification was of effects. Perhaps he was suggesting little more than a commonsense distinction between knowing what to do and knowing how to do it. He informed Lytton Bulwer, for instance, that the proposition 'Morality is an Art, not a Science' is 'merely what everybody thinks, expressed in new language'.[46] But whatever the true rationale, the distinction made it feasible for Mill to talk of the same subject as both art and science. Ethics or morals, for instance, 'so far as it consists of the theory of the moral sentiments, and the investigation of those conditions of human well-being, disclosed by experience, is, in all senses of the word, a science'; but the 'rules or precepts of morals are an art'. A similar argument could be applied to politics. Politics was undoubtedly a science when it was concerned with 'the laws of political phenomena; it is a science of human nature under social conditions'. As an art, however, politics was made up 'of rules, founded on the science, for the right guidance and government of the affairs of society'.[47] Unfortunately, Mill failed to enlarge on this argument, but his distinction between theoretical and practical knowledge obviously removed the possibility of politics being considered as solely a theoretical or scientific subject. Science was not capable of providing knowledge of the ends to be pursued. This province belonged exclusively to art or practice, and while there might well be a science of politics as part of a general science of society, those parts of politics which had to do with the effects of actions, such as legislation and policy making, were bound to remain matters of art, not matters of science.

This is clearly an issue of some importance. If we take Mill's distinction between art and science to be a distinction between ends and means, then it was quite impossible for him to accept authorities on how to live. Questions about ends were all matters of opinion and not matters of fact, and on these questions no person should defer to the expertise or authority of another. A person could recognise the value of other ends, of course; he might even see these ends as better than his own in some sense or senses. But the ability to do this rested upon those qualities which unthinking deference to the authority of science would either prevent or stifle. Authority and expertise, then, could only be properly applied to arguments about means; arguments, that is, which turned upon matters of fact. And even here such arguments supposed sufficient agreement about ends to make debate about means worthwhile. At the end of the day, Mill was always inclined to stick to a very simple point. Arguments about means were not capable of resolving arguments about ends. While it was perfectly proper for the eclectic to reduce the number of appeals to ultimate ends or final principles, he should never pretend that agreement about ends could proceed from the kind of knowledge for which conclusive proofs might be given. In politics, as in all arts, there was no point in searching for more certainty than was possible.

We also need to add a word about changes in Mill's views on unanimity. We have suggested that almost as soon as Mill realised unanimity brought political advantages, he began to question the possibility of such agreement in science and to limit its application to technical questions. Granted the right of private judgement and the need for free discussion on matters of opinion, the instructed few were no more likely to agree about political questions than any other group in society. In the early and middle thirties, it is very possible he thought differently. The Saint-Simonian influence was strong. The Coleridgean clerisy remained an ideal. Also, as a practical eclectic searching for areas of compromise and for common *axiomata media*, Mill tended to disparage disagreement and to look to physical science to end useless controversies. At this time, like Comte himself, he was very prone to attribute difference of opinion in science either to simple prejudice or to an incomplete methodology. Once theology and metaphysics had been expelled, knowledge would become positive, science would be complete, and all those instructed correctly would agree. The many would then be able to defer with quiet confidence.

This view was most marked in the early and middle years of the thirties. But, even at this time, Mill still held to his crucial distinction between art and science and insisted upon the right of private judgement. And although the *Logic*, first published in 1843, clearly shows traces of positivism, Comte was considerably less significant to Mill than scientists like Bain, Herschel and Whewell. Indeed, the more Mill knew about positivism, the less he was committed to it. While he always believed in the value of agreement, after the middle thirties he could not see this agreement resulting either from progress in science or from unanimity amongst the scientific élite. It is worth noting, perhaps, that in his final response to positivism in 1865, agreement among scientists had become no more than a pious and somewhat improbable hope. Sociology was too complex and too uncertain for it to be likely that 'two inquirers equally competent and equally disinterested will take the same view of the evidence, or arrive at the same conclusion'. Mill went on: 'when to this intrinsic difficulty is added the infinitely greater extent to which personal or class interests and predilections interfere with impartial judgement, the hope of such accordance of opinion among sociological inquirers as would obtain, in mere deference to their authority, the universal assent which M. Comte's scheme of society requires, must be adjourned to an indefinite distance'.[48]

Our conclusion, then, can be simple. Mill valued unanimity: agreement was an indispensable security for good government, and an intellectually homogeneous society was more likely than any other to enjoy the benefits of responsible government. But Mill did not believe that such unanimity or homogeneity could be derived from the dissemination of a positive science of politics. He may have believed differently in the early and middle thirties: his letters, as well as his writings in the *Examiner*, constantly emphasise the need for consensus. The collective mediocrity of democratic politics needed to be offset by a consensus amongst the intellectual élite, analogous with the agreement it was possible to reach amongst physical scientists. On consideration, however, Mill dismissed this as a practical possibility. Science was just as likely to promote disagreement as agreement. And he was certain that the rules of moral and political conduct could not be held to on the authority of persons other than the agent, no matter greater knowledge or superior insight; the right of private judgement could not be abdicated if self-culture were to proceed. If self-culture did not proceed, then it would be impossible to account for individual responsibility and to generate the disinterested motives essential to social reform. For this reason, free inquiry by all, and not just by some, was indispensable. This explains Mill's treatment of the élite or clerisy. The élite was neither a final repository of truth, nor a guardian of morals; it was a means to the education of the non-élite. And although it could provide standards of conduct and act as an example of virtuous living, it had no power to compel adherence to these standards in the name of 'science'. Hence, for Mill, there was no question of an élite or clerisy organised as a separate ruling group or party controlling opinion and demanding deference from the non-élite. The élite was simply one means of raising the intelligence of the non-élite, and the influence it possessed necessarily excluded compulsion, social disapprobation and legal imposition. The *Inaugural Address* of February 1867 gave just the right emphasis. Mill accepted that a modest and provisional deference was 'becoming in a youthful and imperfectly formed mind'. But, 'whatever you do, keep, at all risks, your minds open: do not barter away your freedom of thought'.[49] There is no doubt about Mill's commitment here.

In fact, despite the suggestions of those commentators who present him as an authoritarian and an élitist, Mill saw freedom of inquiry by everyone as both indispensable and unavoidable. Such freedom was one of 'the needs of modern life' and one of 'the instincts of the modern mind'.[50] The clock could not be put back; neither art nor science could ever again be built on the ignorance of the many. For the élite to be at all effective as a means to education, there had to be a literate, socially mobile and co-operative political culture; one in which interests were associated and common purpose or purposes acted upon. Even with these conditions fulfilled, the authority of the instructed few could never be a consequence of an exact or complete system of science analogous with physics, mechanics or mathematics. In politics, the limitations of time, place and circumstance were permanent. The practitioner was forced to proceed pragmatically, case by case, issue by issue, with whatever certainty was to hand. All appeals, of course, should be to observation and experience, but it was inconceivable that the outcome of such appeals could be determined, either by the application of a single rule, or by dedicated reliance upon the methods of physical science. Mill was far too much of an eclectic to believe in either possibility. Science was a guide to personal judgement, not a substitute for it; and after a brief and limited flirtation with other views, notably with those of Comte and the French Saint-Simonians, Mill never really pretended otherwise. He insisted on 'perfect freedom of discussion in all its modes—speaking, writing, and printing', for one very good reason; it was 'the first condition of popular intelligence and mental progress. All else is secondary. A form of government is good chiefly in proportion to the security it affords for the possession of this'.[51] In short, science was subordinate to liberty. There was no question of accepting the despotism of science for the benefits consensus would bring. This had been Comte's mistake: he had wanted a 'corporate hierarchy' invested with 'spiritual supremacy'; consequently, he had planned 'the completest system of spiritual and temporal despotism, which ever yet emanated from a human brain'.[52] In Mill's view, only Ignatius Loyola had managed to do worse.

Notes Chapter III

1 John Austin, *The Province of Jurisprudence Determined*, 2nd edn (London, John Murray, 1861), Lecture III, pp. 57–62 in particular. Most of those who observe a system of rules, Austin argued, were 'unable to perceive their ends'

and are 'ignorant of the reasons on which they were founded, or of the proofs from which they were inferred'. Mill himself wrote: 'Of all views I have yet seen taken of the utilitarian scheme, I like Austin's best, in his book on *The Province of Jurisprudence*; but even that falls very far short of what is wanted.' Mill to Pringle Nichol, *The Earlier Letters of John Stuart Mill, 1812–1848* (Toronto, Univ. of Toronto Press, 1963), *Collected Works*, vol. XII, p. 236. Mill also gave *The Province* a favourable review in *Tait's Edinburgh Magazine*.

2 'The Rationale of Political Representation', *London and Westminster Review*, vol. I and 30 (*L.R.T.*, *W.R.* XXX), July 1835, p. 348.

3 ibid., p. 349.

4 Mill wrote lengthy and favourable reviews of Tocqueville in 1835 and again in 1840. His first review appeared in the *London and Westminster Review*. Here, Mill argued that 'in the existence of a leisured class, we see the great and salutary corrective of all the inconveniences to which democracy is liable'. 'Tocqueville on Democracy in America', Gertrude Himmelfarb (ed.), *Essays on Politics and Culture* (New York, Doubleday & Co., 1962), p. 210. Several accounts of Mill's response to Tocqueville are readily available, including the useful H. O. Pappé, 'Mill and Tocqueville', *Journal of the History of Ideas*, vol. XXV, no. 2, 1964, pp. 217–34.

5 J. Stillinger (ed.), *Autobiography* (London, O.U.P., 1971), p. 96.

6 Mill to d'Eichthal, *Letters*, op. cit., XII, p. 40.

7 J. F. W. Herschel, *A Preliminary Discourse on the Study of Natural Philosophy* (New York, Johnson Reprint Cor., 1966), facsimile of the 1830 edition, ch. 2, sect. 20, p. 25. Mill's indebtedness to Herschel is now commonly accepted and quite easy to establish: see, for instance, Mill to Herschel, *Letters*, op. cit., XIII, pp. 583–4.

8 *A System of Logic* (London, Longmans, 1970), Introduction, p. 8.

9 ibid., Preface to the first edition, p.v.

10 J. Stillinger (ed.), *The Early Draft of John Stuart Mill's Autobiography* (Urbana, Univ. of Illinois Press, 1961), p. 189.

11 'Tocqueville on Democracy in America', op. cit., p. 197.

12 *Examiner*, 20 March 1831, pp. 179–80, being Mill's review of Herschel's *A Preliminary Discourse*, op. cit. Writing of the perfection of physical science, Mill added: 'It is an example, and the only example, of a vast body of connected truth, gradually elicited by patient and earnest investigation, and finally recognised and submitted to by a convinced and subdued world' (p. 179).

13 Mill to the Rev. Carr, *Letters*, op. cit., XIV, pp. 80–1.

14 Mill's Diary, Hugh Elliot (ed.), *The Letters of John Stuart Mill* (London, Longmans et al., 1910), vol. II, Appendix A, p. 378.

15 Mill to Austin, *Letters*, op. cit., XIII, p. 712. Mill informed Austin: 'I have necessarily thought a good deal about it lately for the purposes of a practical treatise on Pol. Economy.'

16 'On the Definition of Political Economy', *Essays on Economics and Society* (Toronto, Univ. of Toronto Press, 1967), *Collected Works*, vol. IV, p. 312. Alan Ryan is one of the very few commentators to recognise the importance of this essay in the formation of Mill's arguments in the *Logic*: see *The Philosophy of John Stuart Mill* (London, Macmillan & Co., 1970). Karl Britton makes no

SCIENCE AND THE AUTHORITY OF THE INSTRUCTED

reference to the essay in his chapters on 'Deduction and Demonstrative Science' and 'Induction and Scientific Method' in his *John Stuart Mill* (New York, Dover Pub., 1969). The same applies to Reginald Jackson, *An Examination of the Deductive Logic of John Stuart Mill* (London, O.U.P., 1941).

17 'On the Definition of Political Economy', op. cit., pp. 319–20.

18 *Logic*, op. cit., bk VI, ch. XII, sect. 6, p. 619. Mill took the pedigree of his ideas on art back to the *Gorgias* of Plato. 'An art would not be an art, unless it were founded upon a scientific knowledge of the properties of the subject-matter: without this, it would not be philosophy, but empiricism' ('On the Definition of Political Economy', op. cit., p. 312).

19 *Examiner*, 20 March 1831, op. cit., p. 179.

20 'On the Definition of Political Economy', op. cit., p. 338.

21 Karl Popper, *The Logic of Scientific Discovery* (London, Hutchinson, 1959), ch. III, p. 59.

22 *Logic*, op. cit., bk III, ch. XII, p. 311.

23 ibid., pp. 310–11.

24 *Dissertations and Discussions* (London, Parker & Son, 1859), vol. II, p. 511.

25 'Tocqueville on Democracy in America', op. cit., p. 216.

26 Mill to Sterling, *Letters*, op. cit., XIII, p. 412.

27 Mill's Diary, op. cit., p. 366.

28 *Autobiography*, op. cit., pp. 134–5. 'To expel it from these, is to drive it from its stronghold: and because this had never been effectually done, the intuitive school, even after what my father had written in his Analysis of the Mind, had in appearance, and as far as published writings were concerned, on the whole the best of the argument' (p. 135).

29 William Whewell, *The Philosophy of the Inductive Sciences* (New York Johnson Reprint Cor., 1967), facsimile of the second edition, 1847, vol. I, ch. IV, p. 59. Mill acknowledged his indebtedness to Whewell in the preface to the first edition of the *Logic*: 'without the aid derived from the facts and ideas contained in that gentleman's *History of the Inductive Sciences*, the corresponding portion of this work would probably not have been written' (*Logic*, op. cit., p. v).

30 *Logic*, bk VI, ch. VI, sect. 2, p. 573.

31 ibid., III, VI, I, p. 243.

32 ibid., VI, VII, 2, p. 575.

33 ibid., VI, VIII, 3, p. 580.

34 ibid., p. 583.

35 ibid., p. 583.

36 *Dissertations and Discussions*, op. cit., 'Michelet's History of France', pp. 127–8.

37 'Civilization', J. B. Schneewind (ed.), *Mill's Essays on Literature and Society* (New York, Collier-Macmillan, 1965), pp. 180–1.

38 'On the Definition of Political Economy', op. cit., p. 333.

39 *Logic*, op. cit., VI, X, 5, p. 600.

40 ibid., p. 601.

41 ibid., VI, X, 7, p. 607. Unfortunately, Mill does not explain how knowledge could be both complete and also expanding from within. If it is expanding, presumably it is not complete, and if it is complete, then there is no need for expansion. Possibly he meant that there would be agreement about the questions and about what would constitute an answer, even though those answers still needed to be given. In short, 'complete' means 'positive' in Comte's sense.

42 ibid., VI, X, 5, p. 600.

43 *Inaugural Address, Essays on Literature and Society*, op. cit., p. 391. Mill was elected the Lord Rector in 1865. He was too busy as MP for Westminster to take office immediately and his address was not delivered until 1 February 1867. His address is reported to have lasted three hours and to have been well received.

44 'Carlyle's French Revolution', ibid., p. 201.

45 *An Examination of Sir William Hamilton's Philosophy* (London, Longmans, Green & Co., 1889), sixth edition, ch. XX, pp. 449–51.

46 Mill to Bulwer, *Letters*, op. cit., XIII, p. 579.

47 *Sir William Hamilton*, op. cit., p. 449.

48 *Auguste Comte and Positivism* (Ann Arbor, Univ. of Michigan Press, 1961), part 1, p. 121.

49 *Inaugural Address*, op. cit., pp. 400–1.

50 Mill's Diary, op. cit., 6 February, p. 368.

51 ibid., 18 March, p. 379.

52 *Autobiography*, op. cit., p. 127. Comte's *Système de Politique Positive* 'stands a monumental warning to thinkers on society and politics, of what happens when once men lose sight, in their speculations, of the value of Liberty and of Individuality' (pp. 127–8).

Chapter IV

Laissez-faire, Socialism and Future Society

Mill's new utilitarianism which established a primary concern for self-development, his understanding of the relation between authority and free inquiry and his persistent eclectic desire to promote agreement, had all led by the early 1840s to an unambiguous conception of the conditions necessary for free individual agency. It is also worth remembering that Mill himself took his opinions to be fixed by this time. He had 'no further mental changes to tell of, but only, as I hope, a continued mental progress'.[1] He had, indeed, reached some kind of conclusion—a more or less settled understanding of the nature of moral and political philosophy. The fixed points seem obvious enough. Just as increases in happiness were hopeless which were due solely to a change of outward circumstances and not to a change in the state of the desires, so were rules of conduct authoritatively imposed as truths of science. No one could be compelled to be good, any more than he should accept truths he had not seen for himself; and if true or ideal happiness presumed changes of feeling, so the free acceptance of rules of conduct presumed a well-developed state of moral and intellectual culture. The vast majority would neither experience happiness, nor freely accept obligations, without self-education; this, in turn, could not proceed effectively without substantial social and political reforms. The radical party held to this view almost as an article of faith. Mill's 'philosophy of movement' certainly retained some aristocratic emphases, remnants, perhaps, of a tory disdain for the common man, but his notion of education still presumed fairly radical changes in social structure and political institutions. Mill made this clear in a long and patient letter to d'Eichthal. Mankind would not be perfected by instruction or by teaching. Without an alteration in 'those parts of our social institutions and policy which at present oppose improvement, degrade and brutalise the intellects and morality of the people, giving all the ascendancy to mere wealth', there would not be 'the growth of a *pouvoir spirituel* capable of commanding the faith of the majority who must and do believe on authority'.[2] As a radical, Mill assumed the interdependence of reform by individual exertion and reform by public agency. To him, self-culture and social reform were inseparable; an intelligent and active character presumed a responsible society.

It is this belief more than any other which explains Mill's understanding of the two principles or ideologies of *laissez-faire* and socialism, and helps to clarify his conception of future society. Yet the nature of his commitment to these principles has often been misunderstood and misinterpreted, in part, no doubt, as a consequence of Mill's general reputation as an economist. Too often, his writings are approached as if they were designed simply to add bits and pieces to the Ricardian system; this attitude is now less fashionable than it once was, but it is still fairly common. There has also been more persistent misrepresentation of these views than of others. Many commentators, for instance, are content to present the *laissez-faire* principle as a narrow economic argument in favour of free trade and the free market, identifying the doctrine with an unrestrained business ethic. Others find Mill's socialism very puzzling, wondering whether he meant 'a centralised organisation run by an all-powerful state, or more nearly a form of syndicalism'.[3] One thing is absolutely certain: Mill never saw the choice in those terms at all. To some extent, possibly, Mill himself is to blame for these ambiguities of interpretation. He never completed the book on socialism which had been in his mind for over twenty years. Instead, he left one or two chapters which were only published six years after his death. His major work on economic theory, the *Principles of Political Economy*, was subject to more or less constant revision. Seven library editions appeared between 1848 and Mill's death in 1873; there was also a single-volume people's edition which was frequently reissued, and all of these editions embodied changes, some of which were substantial. No one can be certain, either, about Harriet Taylor's role in making Mill more receptive to socialist ideas—there has been a great deal of inconclusive discussion about this, to which we need not add—but she certainly persuaded him to tone down the criticisms he had made of Owenism in the first edition of the *Principles*; indeed, her commitment to co-operative socialism seems to have been charged with an emotion entirely lacking in her personal relationships. Nor is the *Autobiography* much help on these matters: there are clear differences between the various drafts in all of the passages dealing with Mill's response to socialism. This chapter is an attempt to clear up some of these doubts and confusions by relating Mill's understanding of *laissez-faire* and socialism more carefully to his moral and political philosophy. We can begin with the *laissez-faire* principle itself. In the first instance, we may offer a simple and unrefined characterisation.

With Mill, the principle did not limit the province of government 'to the protection of person and property against force and fraud'. He rejected this notion out of hand in the *Principles*; already in the essay on 'Coleridge', published eight years before the first edition of the *Principles*, he had represented the 'let alone' doctrine as 'generated by the manifest selfishness and incompetence of modern European governments'.[4] The origins of the 'let alone' doctrine are somewhat elusive. Usually, it is taken to be a common eighteenth-century understanding of *laissez-faire*, associated most perhaps with Smith, Mandeville and the Physiocrats.[5] But each examination of the classical economists' views on policy, whether of Ricardo on monetary matters, or of Nassau Senior on factory legislation, seems to throw up exceptions to a policy of 'let alone'.[6] There was, all the same, a marked tendency in some eighteenth-century thinkers to subordinate political to social phenomena. Society was conceived as an autonomous and efficient unity, analogous either with a healthy body or with an efficient machine. This unity required no external political direction and no detailed public administration. The distribution of benefits which followed as an unintended consequence of individual agency in any case brought about a result very close to that which a rational legislator would seek to bring about. A natural or spontaneous distribution, in short, was just as fair as any contrived or artificial balance of benefits. Left to itself, individual agency in pursuit of self-interest would achieve a rough measure of justice, a degree of equality, and it would also provide the conditions for further economic growth. On this view, consequently, there was always a presumption against political interference except where that was designed to protect person and property against force and fraud. The object of justice was security, and justice was the foundation of all civil government. No ruler need contemplate more. The laws of natural justice were laws of non-interference. The conclusion to this argument was simple: that government is best which governs least.

Whether or not the origins were elusive, Mill himself was very familiar with this 'let alone' conception of the *laissez-faire* principle. Coleridge had already made his own rejection of this conception public, and Mill advised Cairnes to extend his examination of Bastiat's economic ideas just to 'show how far from the truth it is that the economic phenomena of a society as at present constituted always arrange themselves spontaneously in the way which is most for the common good'.[7] In 1832 Mill supported a proposal to limit the work of women and children in factories. In doing so, he felt bound to reject all of those arguments drawn from 'the non-interference philosophy, and resting on the maxim, that government ought not to prohibit individuals, not under the influence of force and fraud, from binding themselves by any engagement which they may think fit to contract'.[8] There are many more examples of his familiarity with this view, all of which leave no doubt where Mill stood. For Mill, *laissez-faire* was not synonymous with 'let alone'. The principle was neither an absolute nor an automatic argument against political interference. He quite clearly regarded the common eighteenth-century understanding of *laissez-faire* as far too narrow and prohibitive. There are several reasons why this was likely to be the case. Mill's new utilitarianism did not require a belief in final truths of human nature. Consequently, no such truths existed to limit the province of government: human nature and government were both variable. And Mill always adopted a pragmatic attitude: problems should be handled as they came along, issue by issue, case by case. Being an eclectic also, Mill preferred to avoid final principles and single ends. The 'let alone' conception was too likely to make compromise impossible. All these reasons have been touched on before, but there is also Mill's indebtedness to Tocqueville which must not be forgotten. This was crucially important in the development of his opinions on *laissez-faire* and it needs to be considered in some detail. The *Autobiography* provides many clues.

While Tocqueville undoubtedly gave an urgency to Mill's misgivings about government by the numerical and ignorant majority, confirming his persistent tory doubts about the masses and highlighting 'the specific dangers which beset Democracy', the *Autobiography* also shows that Mill leant heavily on Tocqueville for his views on centralisation. By his own admission, this was the 'collateral subject' on which he 'derived great benefit from the study of Tocqueville'.[9] The analysis of America's egalitarian and loosely federated society established the political importance of local institutions. The popular defence of centralisation, that it was the only efficient form of government possible for a civilised society, preventing the abuses of shambling despotisms, was put in serious doubt. And Tocqueville's understanding of the importance of the 'practical political activity' of the people in performing as much of 'the collective business of society, as can safely be so performed', impressed Mill greatly. His assessment of Tocqueville's findings on centralisation was one of the foundations of his own interpretation of the *laissez-faire* principle. Stated simply, it amounted to a belief that the training of one's own conduct through practical participation made possible participation in a responsible political system. The 'practical political activity of the individual citizen' was 'one of the most effectual means of training the social feelings and practical intelligence of the people'. This kind of elevated intelligence was indispensable to good government. But it was also 'the specific counteractive to some of the characteristic infirmities of democracy, and a necessary protection against it degenerating into the only despotism of which, in the modern world, there is a real danger—the absolute rule of the head of the executive over a congregation of isolated individuals, all equals but all slaves'.[10]

This is plain enough. In Mill's view, free government required the public education of the citizens. 'Practical political activity', or participation, was crucial since it made possible for each participant a development of social feeling, as well as a growth in intelligence and imagination. In effect, Mill's ideology of *laissez-faire* amounted to a defence of voluntary participation and of decentralisation with the problems of self-culture and social education very much in mind. Not surprisingly, then, it seems to have been Tocqueville's analysis of American society and government which led Mill to advocate a scheme whereby the whole country would be covered with small sub-parliaments, to which the local executives would be accountable; a scheme of local self-government originally put forward in the *Examiner*.[11] Mill also acknowledged one other effect in the *Autobiography* which was very welcome to an eclectic. The 'lessons of Tocqueville' had stopped him from going to extremes. When he had first read Tocqueville, Mill was busy defending various measures such as the 'Poor Law Reform of 1834, against an irrational clamour grounded on the Anti-Centralisation prejudice'. Without Tocqueville's influence, 'I do not know that I might not, like many reformers before me, have been hurried into the excess opposite to that which, being the one prevalent in my own country, it was generally my business to combat'.[12] In fact, when Mill first met Tocqueville in 1835, and before he had begun a systematic study of his writings, he was not greatly impressed by arguments in favour of local government and municipal institutions. Like all radicals of that time, Mill saw local politics as the politics of corruption and influence. Tocqueville recalled Mill's view that 'the present communal and provincial institutions' were instruments of the aristocracy. To vest substantive powers in these institutions was only to perpetuate oligarchic rule. Consequently, Mill favoured central against local government; 'when we take away this power from our adversaries, we naturally think of vesting it in the government, since there is nothing ready in the present institutions to inherit this power'.[13] After his study of Tocqueville, this could no longer be Mill's attitude, and his attachment to the *laissez-faire* principle took on a much more definite shape.

After his reading of Tocqueville, Mill's adherence to the *laissez-faire* principle did not presume a belief in irreversible market laws or in fixed standards of economic behaviour justified as either 'natural' or 'spontaneous'. There were no final truths about human nature. Like any good pragmatist, Mill firmly denied that the principle supplied either a universal theory of human behaviour, or a complete argument about the limits of government intervention. The 'wise practitioner', as Mill noted in the *Logic*, regarded all rules of conduct as provisional and recognised the error of attempting to deduce specific policies from 'supposed universal practical maxims'.[14] Hence, those cases falling broadly under the *laissez-faire* principle could not be solved by the application of a single rule. No one should pretend that a belief in the principle supposed a universal solution to all of the problems of non-interference. To Mill, the whole point of the principle was to indicate those circumstances in which individual initiative and voluntary experiment might be encouraged and made effective without being made legally obligatory. The chapters dealing with *laissez-faire* in the *Principles* stated the idea simply enough. 'The ground of the practical principle of non-interference' was precisely 'that most persons take a juster and more intelligent view of their own interest, and that of the means of promoting it, than can either be prescribed to them by a general enactment of the legislature, or pointed out in the particular case by a public functionary'.[15] Quite simply, on the question of what he wants and how to get it, each man himself was the best judge; no one could determine another person's wants for him. It followed that a man's interests were to be defined as those conditions necessary to satisfy wants. A commitment to *laissez-faire*, then, entailed only two initial assumptions: first, that all people were creatures of wants; second, that they were active and intelligent in pursuit of their interests.

This notion of an active and intelligent citizenry in pursuit of wants was the most basic presupposition of *laissez-faire*, and this activity was thought to be facilitated by high levels of participation. Taking part in action, or having a share with others in some action, was seen as part of a process of political and moral education. The training of character which resulted from practical participatory activity was indispensable, not only in making the choices of individuals responsible choices, but also in ensuring the overall responsibility of the political system. As Mill once remarked: 'it is difficult to imagine what theory of education that can be, which can attach no importance to such an instrument'. The 'mental faculties will be most developed where they are most exercised'.[16] In Mill's view as well, a commitment to *laissez-faire* was also a commitment to self-culture. A person's vision was expanded and judgements were refined. The individual developed himself, making his social conduct more responsible and his own character more enlightened. Mill always retained enough of the two-part theory of morality to believe in an interdependence of character and conduct. The means to this improvement of character and conduct were many and varied. A high rate of popular access to local administrative institutions, a wide range of functions for municipal government and a redistribution of landed property were the means Mill emphasised most often. The smaller commonwealths of antiquity, notably that of Athens, were often in his mind here. The Athenian notion that a man removed from public life was in some very real sense 'useless' and less than a man was quite close to his own view. As an eclectic, however, Mill was unwilling to rule out any practical possibility or to veto any kind of social experiment. Voluntary participation and local political decentralisation might properly take many forms. There was no point in ruling out any of these *a priori* since the whole basis of *laissez-faire* was wide and varied experiment. After this simple and preliminary definition of *laissez-faire*, we can turn to the socialist principle. Here again, we need a simple and unrefined characterisation to begin with.

To Mill, the socialist principle was incompatible with the pursuit of merely material ends or objects. The appetites of man should be altered and improved, not merely confirmed, and the reorganisation of production ought not to be made the single or ultimate end of the social union. This was one of Mill's strongest objections to Saint-Simonian socialism and to Comte's social philosophy. Comte recognised only two ends: 'the dominion of man over man, which is conquest', and 'the dominion of man over nature, which is production'. To Mill, this showed the origins of the theory: 'the St. Simon philosophy could only originate in France. If M. Comte were a native of England, where this idol "production" has been set up and worshipped with incessant devotion for a century back', then he would have seen 'how the disproportionate importance attached to it lies at the root of all our worst national vices, corrupts the measures of our statesmen, the doctrines of our philosophers and hardens the minds of our people so as to make it almost hopeless to inspire them with any elevation either of intellect or of soul'.[17] This is very strong condemnation indeed. And when Mill became fully aware of Saint-Simonian proposals for the distribution of benefits and for the grading of occupations by a central administrative authority, he ceased to regard the Saint-Simonian version of socialism as either desirable or feasible. In his view, the socialist principle should not entail the permanent public administration of material welfare. State management should not become a rule, or even a confirmed practice, but rather an exceptional resort to be justified in each particular case. This pragmatic and non-dogmatic approach was more marked, perhaps, after the revolutions of 1848. The hostility of English opinion to European socialism and the reaction of the parties of order, convinced Mill that for socialism to be tried as an experiment it would have to be established through a series of piecemeal approximations. Indeed,

JOHN STUART MILL

this was the main conclusion to be drawn from Mill's defence of the French socialists against the attacks of Lord Brougham, a defence which appeared in the *Westminster Review* in April 1849.[18]

Presumably, this was a consistent if not necessarily a correct attitude for Mill to adopt: a confirmed eclectic could hardly think otherwise. Like any other single principle, socialism could never guarantee a monopoly of truth for any one means of social and economic reform. Social and economic experiment, what Mill called the 'testing' of social theories and economic ideas, was educational. As such, it was indispensable. But this very fact made the adoption of any one social theory or any one economic idea as final truth impossible. The socialist principle, in his sense, did not contain a detailed prescription for all courses of conduct, nor did the principle establish a complete programme of action for all foreseeable circumstances. Such prescriptions and programmes were no more possible in social and economic policy than they were in moral and political philosophy. One always had to learn by trial and error, balancing success against failure, and every theory was limited by the means available for its application. To pretend otherwise, was the most arrant and narrow dogmatism. In his 'Speech on Mr. Maguire's Motion on the State of Ireland', Mill reminded everyone of his views on political economy. Political economy, he maintained, was 'a science by means of which we are enabled to form a judgement as to what each particular case requires; but it does not supply us with a ready-made judgement upon any case, and there cannot be a greater enemy to political economy then he who represents it in that light'.[19] This is the familiar language of the pragmatist. In general, of course, Mill was prepared to recommend any scheme for adoption which would abolish great differentials in wealth while demonstrating an ability to co-operate for mutual benefit. At one time or another, he supported industrial partnership, profit sharing and piece work as practical socialist 'schools' in which a more general social co-operation could be learnt and then disseminated. As chairman of the Land Tenure Reform Association, Mill also worked for the removal of the law of primogeniture, the limitation or prohibition of increased private land holding and for heavy taxes on unearned increment from land,[20] although, unlike members of the Land and Labour League, he did not advocate land nationalisation. As is well known, he also supported the redistribution of land in Ireland in the form of small peasant holdings.

Obviously, the particular emphasis varied with time and circumstance; a dominant concern at one moment becoming a secondary consideration at another. Mill's belief in peasant proprietorship, for instance, was probably strongest in the years of the late forties. His commitment to this particular system of land tenure first began when he saw it as a solution to the problem of Irish poverty—this is clear in his treatment of proprietorship in the *Principles*—and he ran several campaigns, often flecked with bad temper, in the forties and in his two years as MP for Westminster between 1866 and 1868 to secure the adoption of this system. Indeed, Mill was offered the chance to contest a rural Irish county largely as a consequence of his views on proprietorship. But whatever the time and circumstance, and whatever the particular policy recommendation, there can be no doubt about the nature of Mill's general commitment. While he was capable of great irritation at the ordinary intelligence of the masses, he also valued equality, not instrumentally, but as an end in itself. He informed Arthur Helps, for instance, that he looked upon 'inequality as *in itself* always an evil'. 'I do not agree with any one who would use the machinery of society for the purpose of promoting it.'[21] Also, in his defence of the 1848 revolution in France and of the Provisional Government, he was prepared to identify himself with Bentham on this point. While admitting to a distrust of some of the means socialists proposed for effecting social change, he left no doubt about the end.

> 'We hold with Bentham, that equality, though not the sole end, is one of the ends of good social arrangements: and that a system of institutions which does not make the scale turn in favour of equality, whenever this can be done without impairing the security of the property which is the product and reward of personal exertion, is essentially a bad government—a government for the few, to the injury of the many.'[22]

This passage, however, indicates our first main difficulty. A scale of priorities is clearly implied, and those priorities seem to favour the institution of private property above the end of equality. For some commentators, this is sufficient to disqualify Mill as a socialist, making his egalitarian claims either misleading or dishonest.[23]

The point is arguable. To some extent, no doubt, the matter is a semantic one. If by socialist we mean 'revolutionary', then Mill was not a socialist. He consistently opposed the use of force to effect social change: class domination, he considered, would not be ended by violence. In his *Posthumous Chapters on Socialism*, he even suggested that the sole motivation of revolutionary socialists was hate, and his response to the First International was to distinguish between the English socialists, who were concerned with practical amelioration, and Continental socialists full of hatred and violence towards the proprietary classes. If, on the other hand, by socialist we mean an opponent of the institution of private property, then Mill again was not a socialist. The third edition of the *Principles of Political Economy* concluded very strongly in favour of private property and competition. Indeed, Mill ended the redrafted chapter on Property by stating 'that the object to be principally aimed at in the present stage of human improvement, is not the subversion of the system of individual property, but the improvement of it, and in the full participation of every member of the community in its benefits', although he had been careful to add that he was not 'attempting to limit the ultimate capabilities of human nature'.[24] If, finally, a socialist has to hold to his beliefs as a complete and final system, then, just as clearly again, Mill could not be called a socialist. No eclectic could be. But all of these seem to be unnecessarily stipulative definitions. While there is no doubt that Mill's enthusiasm for socialism tended to cool down after the death of Harriet Taylor, there is also no doubt about the sentiments expressed in the *Autobiography*. Mill believed in socialist experiments. He saw social change not as optional but necessary. He stood by equality. He proposed serious reforms in the competitive system. His opposition to unearned increment was vehement. And if he could never quite overcome his doubts about all of the varieties of the socialist principle, from Owenism to Fourierism, this was true of all the principles he encountered. Mill was by nature a sceptic. Quite rightly, he refused to suspend disbelief whether he was faced with conservatism or with socialism.

There is a further difficulty as well. As we have defined them, the principles of *laissez-faire* and socialism were not only compatible, each was essential to the other and both were necessary if Mill was to avoid an understanding of politics as a merely legislative and administrative operation. Those used to seeing a stark contrast between the ideologies of *laissez-faire* and socialism will find this puzzling, but the logic of Mill's position is clear once it is stated. If voluntary participation and co-operative social experiments did educate individual character and improve social conduct, then in Mill's view there would be less need for legal sanctions and for the central administration of material benefits. Individuals would take their social obligations more seriously and would be less concerned to maximise their immediate material wants. This voluntary recognition of common purpose or purposes would tend to preclude or to prevent an unreasoned adherence to economic customs. Consequently, the possibility of disruptive competition between sectional groups or interests would be diminished. Society would be 'conscience' rather than 'class' based. The idol of production would then no longer remain unchallenged, while the benefits of competition could be spread so as to promote distributive ideals like equality. For Mill himself, then, there was no antithesis between *laissez-faire* and socialism; both ideologies were means to a similar end and both were integral parts of the same doctrine of social and political education. Even so, there is a problem about compatibility and sameness. As we have defined them, the principles of *laissez-faire* and socialism are not only compatible, they are also very difficult to distinguish. And for the sake of clarity, we have to distinguish between the two principles more carefully than we have done so far.

The crucial *laissez-faire* distinction was between two types of optional government interference which differed in their nature and effects and in the 'motives' which could justify them. This was the contentious area. There was no problem about those functions of the State which all agreed were necessary for the maintenance of social living. It was only the optional aspect which raised problems, and here Mill distinguished between 'authoritative' and 'non-authoritative' optional interventions. The 'authoritative' interference of government was intervention by sanction, prohibition and legal proscription. These were interventions which extended to controlling the free agency of individuals. All such interventions tended 'to starve the development of some portion of the bodily or mental faculties, either sensitive or active'.[25] Unauthoritative or 'non-authoritative' interference, on the other hand, presumed voluntary enterprise and the responsible use of free agency. Here, intervention or interference was limited to the provision of information and advice, and to the provision of supplementary agencies to complement those established by individual initiative. Mill gave as examples a State system of education, or a Church establishment; these were both cases in which the State favoured institutions of its choosing, but did not prevent individuals from pursuing other religious or educational ends. Mill himself was convinced that 'authoritative' intervention, intervention by sanction, prohibition and proscription, had a far more limited sphere of legitimate action than the other kind of intervention. In practice, then, the important distinction was between legally and administratively dominant central bodies, able to intervene by law and command, and efficient and popular local or municipal agencies which worked because of the free and voluntary endeavours of individuals. Mill obviously thought the progress of civilisation required increases in legislation, but he denied the implication of an increase in central bureaucracy or 'authoritative' government. His essay on 'Centralization' in the *Edinburgh Review* stated that precise point: 'Extension of legislation in itself implies no fresh delegation of power to the executive, no discretionary authority, still less control, still less obligation to ask permission of the executive for every new undertaking[26]'. There could be both over-legislation and over-administration. The one, however, did not necessarily entail the other and neither was, in itself, an argument for 'authoritative' interference, which required justification on grounds of absolute necessity. In this very precise sense, the *laissez-faire* principle supported 'unauthoritative' government and was a positive argument in favour of delegating services and functions to individual, local and municipal agencies. *Laissez-faire*, in fact, was an ideology of local self-government, presuming high levels of popular participation.

One other point should be made. Mill was clear that both 'authoritative' and 'non-authoritative' optional intervention by government depended not upon individual choice *per se*, but upon a particular kind of choice. While each individual was the best judge of what he wanted and how to get it, the *laissez-faire* principle could only have validity if those choices were responsible choices. 'Non-authoritative' government, for instance, in its function of establishing complementary agencies, did leave individuals free, but only 'free to use their own means of pursuing any object of [general] interest'.[27] 'Authoritative' government, on the other hand, could only avoid 'the degradation of slavery' if 'the conscience of the individual goes freely with the legal restraint'. Mill continued:

> 'Scarcely any degree of utility, short of absolute necessity, will justify a prohibitory regulation, unless it can also be made to recommend itself to the general conscience; unless persons of ordinary good intentions either believe already, or can be induced to believe, that the thing prohibited is a thing which they ought not to wish to do.'[28]

His meaning is clear. Just as the free agency of individuals presumed a responsible use of that agency, so the free agency of governments in optional interventions required the existence of responsible choices, or at least the ability to assist in the formation of such choices. Mill had seen this very point in Coleridge's rejection of the 'let alone' doctrine of government. If there was a case for the free agency of individuals, then there was also bound to be a case for the free agency of governments. And he quoted a lengthy passage from the 'Second Lay Sermon', which defined the 'positive ends' of the State, in his 1840 essay on 'Coleridge'. The third and final positive end of the State was the 'development of those faculties which are essential to his humanity, that is, to his rational and moral being'.[29] For Mill, then, free choice meant choices which persons of 'ordinary good intentions' had already made, or choices which they ought to make; using the language of Coleridge, choices essential to their 'rational and moral being'.

Once this point is made about Mill's notion of choice, some of the difficulties apparent in his own personal commitments can be resolved. No one questions the extent and the seriousness of his neo-Malthusianism for instance, though there are doubts about his precise role in distributing birth control propaganda. It is quite common, however, for commentators to present this concern to limit population growth by physical means as standing well outside of the *laissez-faire* principle. Sometimes, in fact, Mill is accused of being a Malthusian fanatic who was quite prepared to invoke 'the tyranny of opinion' to decrease the size of families in the urban labouring class and amongst the agricultural poor. This is unfair since his arguments on the limitation of population, in the *Principles* at least, are perfectly compatible with the *laissez-faire* doctrine and explicable in terms of his general understanding of government intervention. The argument is this.

'If the opinion were once generally established among the labouring class that their welfare required a due regulation of the numbers of families, the respectable and well-conducted of the body would conform to the prescription, and only those would exempt themselves from it, who were in the habit of making light of social obligations generally; and there would be then an evident justification for converting the moral obligation against bringing children into the world who are a burden to the community, into a legal one.'[30]

As we understand it, this is the argument of *laissez-faire* coloured by Mill's pragmatism. Authoritative government intervention is justified in creating a legal obligation in two clear cases: first, where responsible choices have actually been made and common agreement exists; secondly, as is the case with those 'in the habit of making light of social obligations', when a choice or choices have not been made which ought to have been made. This is crucial. *Laissez-faire* was not a principle attaching value solely to free and unhindered choice. This was never Mill's contention. There was also a value attaching to a responsible individuality which should be encouraged in all ways possible, short of compelling individuals to act and to think in certain ways. Here again, the prime commitment is to self-culture and to all of those processes whereby personal motives are elevated and refined, so increasing the likelihood of responsible choices at least amongst the majority. Now, perhaps, we can turn again to the socialist principle.

Correctly understood, the socialist principle was opposed to the permanent control or public administration of welfare on the grounds of free inquiry and self-dependence. People had to think for themselves; they had to manage their affairs by trial and error, relying upon their own exertions. Mill was quick to be angered by any kind of superficial philanthropy; as far as he was concerned, such philanthropy always smacked of paternalism, either implying the incompetence or the irrationality of the lower class. The belief that the more fortunate higher classes should take care of the less fortunate lower classes was totally unacceptable to him. A kind of paternalist and upper-class philanthropy had, in fact, grown up in England in the early and middle forties. This had been keenly sponsored by *The Times*;[31] the polite establishment was favourable, and there were close associations with the Oxford Movement. Mill was inclined to interpret this philanthropy as a political tactic of the rich. The rich were now solicitous and caring because of the threat of Chartism. They clearly hoped to take the steam out of radicalism and out of the Anti-Corn Law League. Mill noted sarcastically that 'English benevolence can no longer be accused of confining itself to niggers and other distant folks'.[32] He was also sure that the effects had been disastrous. 'I never remember a time when any suggestion of anti-population doctrine or of forethought and self-command on the part of the poor was so contemptuously scouted as it is now.' The working class now believed that 'it is other people's business to take care of them'.[33] It was this kind of philanthropy, implying the passive acceptance of a dependent role, which Mill flatly denied when he examined the claims of paternalism in the *Principles*, and in an article, 'The Claims of Labour', published in the *Edinburgh Review* in April 1845, Mill imputed the very worst of motives to the Church paternalists or 'State Puseyites'. They were busy asserting the right of the poor to assistance and protection in the hope that a kind of feudal obedience would follow. Mill was convinced that philanthropic paternalism had 'never existed between human beings, without immediate degradation to the character of the dependent class'. With paternal care inevitably came paternal authority. The deference of the dependent to the superior class was 'either hypocrisy or servility. Real attachment, a genuine feeling of subordination, must now be the result of personal qualities, and requires them on both sides equally'.[34]

Mill drew lasting conclusions from his experience of philanthropic paternalism in the forties. The permanent dispensation of material benefits, whether by a public institution or by the beneficence of a ruling class, would not only encourage the growth of an authoritative central bureaucracy, but it would also encourage the pursuit of merely material ends or objects. The inducements to self-improvement would be lessened, individual initiative would be relied upon less and less and a wholly false system of authority would be widely disseminated. In effect, the practice of paternalism confirmed the worst traits of the national character, while consolidating the pernicious tendencies of the predominance of masses over individuals. Paternalism bred a dull, uninspired and passive conformism. This was Mill's strongest fear also about the ethos of co-operative socialist communities. In reply to a defence of 'the communistic principle', for instance, which had made use of his own arguments in the *Principles*, he stated his fears very bluntly. 'I fear that the yoke of conformity would be made heavier instead of lighter; that people would be compelled to live as it pleased others, not as it pleased themselves; that their lives would be placed under rules, the same for all, prescribed by the majority and that there would be no escape.'[35] Obviously, Mill saw nothing in any of the many varieties of socialism to relieve this fear. Several times he announced his belief in a very simple test for all schemes of welfare and assistance: 'Is the assistance of such a kind, and given in such a manner, as to render them ultimately independent of the continuance of similar assistance?'[36] Independence of mind, energy of character and an active self-culture were the basic values: socialism and freedom could only be reconciled if they were accepted as such. 'To suppose, therefore, that Government will do, better than individuals, anything which individuals are able and willing to do, is to suppose that the average of society is better than any individual in it, which is both a mathematical and a moral absurdity.'[37] This passage alone indicates that Mill had no desire at all for a centralised or state socialism.

When stated in this way, the principles of *laissez-faire* and socialism were clearly compatible for Mill, but they were obviously not the same. *Laissez-faire* was an active defence of all kinds of practical participation and a strong presumption in favour of local and municipal institutions. Socialism amounted to an advocacy of social experiment and to a defence of any means to social co-operation which improved conduct and character, while mitigating the pernicious effects of wage-labour, private ownership and free competition. Purists may object to the words, but whatever one chooses to call these beliefs, whether 'socialist', 'radical-individualist', or more vulgarly, 'bourgeois', they are certainly not out of line with Mill's general understanding of morals and politics. Indeed, they confirm that understanding in all significant respects. Neither principle was held to as a matter of final or complete faith, and neither principle excluded an appeal to secondary or intermediate maxims. For Mill, neither *laissez-faire* nor socialism was a complete policy or theory in itself; such theories were not possible without an unacceptable dogmatism. If social and political experiment was educational, making possible an improvement in personal conduct and in social co-operation, then there was simply no way of telling the final outcome. Many futures were conceivable. For this very reason, no one should be dogmatic in committing himself to one experiment rather than another. This pragmatic and pluralist attitude gave consistency to all that Mill wrote. He never wavered in his view that experiments in education, which included experiments in social structures, ruled out dogmatism. Self-culture was hard work and it brought no final certainties. Consequently, social education was bound to advance very slowly, making its inroads piecemeal. The *Posthumous Chapters*, all that Mill wrote of his book on socialism, gave his considered opinion. 'The education of human beings is one of the most difficult of all arts': improvements 'in general education are necessarily very gradual, because the future generation is educated by the present, and the imperfections of the teachers set an invincible limit to the degree in which they can train their pupils to be better than themselves'.[38] So while there were many possible futures, the limits of those possibilities were always set in the present. A variety of experiments, then, was not only essential in present circumstances, but also for the sake of future human achievement.

To some extent, perhaps, the peculiar quality of the way Mill handled the principles of *laissez-faire* and socialism, a quality which has regularly puzzled his interpreters, derived from his very strong defence of competition and his equally strong disdain for the economics of growth and expansion. He had never been inspired by commercialism and he always tended to emphasise the heavy costs of economic growth. Like Coleridge, he took the commercial spirit to be grubby and sordid, lacking in imagination and bereft of decent ideals. The English worship of production was certainly nothing to be proud of; the whole nation was deadened by it. Mill's high-minded and contemplative toryism had also led him to despise competition for personal gain. While competition was necessary to prevent monopoly, to keep wages high and to prevent idleness and 'mental dullness', it was not to be considered as an end in itself. A life of competition was bound to be sordid and squalid. Mill openly confessed, 'I am not charmed with the ideal of life held out by those who think that the normal state of human beings is that of struggling to get on'.[39] And, in his attempted refutation of Carlyle's arguments on the rights of negroes in *Fraser's Magazine*, Mill scorned the whole gospel of work and competition. The 'multiplication of work, for purposes not worth caring about, is one of the evils of our present condition'; the gospel of work was no more than a 'cant'. In opposition to it, 'I would assert the gospel of leisure, and maintain that human beings *cannot* rise to the finer attributes of their nature compatibly with a life filled with labour'. Like Marx, Mill saw the reduction in the length of the working day as a necessary condition for the individual to become free, and to 'reduce very greatly the quantity of work required to carry on existence, is as needful as to distribute it more equally'.[40] This article scorning the work ethic was published in 1850, and reflects the continuing influence of Wordsworth and the romantics. Obviously, Mill had remembered the lesson he had learnt from those eclectic spirits: happiness was perfectly compatible with contemplation and 'may coexist with being stationary and does not require us to keep moving'.[41]

The best known continuation of this romantic and tory critique of work and competition, however, is the chapter on the 'Stationary State' in the *Principles*. Very few changes were made to this chapter throughout the seven editions, and it was obviously intended as a kind of pro-legomenon to a more detailed statement on future possibilities. The chapter 'On the Probable Futurity of the Labouring Classes' was not included in the first manuscript draft of the *Principles* and was only added at the insistence of Harriet Taylor. Indeed, the notion of a 'Stationary State', where men have ceased to accumulate material wealth, co-operating instead in the pursuit of more elevated ends, is a close approximation to Mill's vision of future society. Like many other Victorians, Mill seems to have believed that genuinely creative activity takes place only outside or beyond the competitive system of industrial production. In his reply to Carlyle, he had bitterly condemned 'the exhausting, stiffening, stupefying toil of many kinds of agricultural and manufacturing labourers', advocating a substantial reduction in the length of the working day. In the chapter on the 'Stationary State', he made no apology for being 'comparatively indifferent to the kind of economical progress which excites the congratulations of ordinary politicians; the mere increase of production and accumulation'.[42] A 'stationary' or 'no-growth' state of capital and population was perfectly compatible with human improvement. Mental and moral culture would have just as much scope for improvement, if not more. In fact, the 'Art of Living' would be more likely to be improved 'when minds ceased to be engrossed by the art of getting on'.[43] Other men would no longer be regarded as either enemies or competitors, interests could then be associated and common purpose or purposes recognised. If 'stationari-ness' could exist with rising incomes, with constant technological in-novation and with a reduction in the length of the working day, then Mill was convinced that it would be better to choose 'stationariness' rather than growth, 'long before necessity' compelled that choice anyway.[44]

One other condition would have to be met, however, before 'station-ariness' would be preferable to any other condition. Growth in numbers would have to be checked. High living standards upon the basis of a shorter working day could only be protected if this were the case. Without control of population growth and family size, man could not be liberated from the excesses of work and competition; scarcity would never be overcome. Time and time again, from the early twenties until the end of his life, Mill emphasised that the good society required population to be brought under 'the deliberate guidance of judicious foresight'. His own views on female emancipation reflected this concern for birth control: the guidance would be more deliberate and more judicious once the social and political emancipation of women was complete, since women would then no longer be confined to the one 'animal' function. Mill's own ideal future condition was obviously founded on a prejudice against the costs of economic growth. For this reason, many of his criticisms of industrial society and the work ethic smack of modern 'environmentalist' arguments. Nature was constantly ransacked for greater and greater production. Species other than man were plundered and destroyed. The countryside was radically altered and lessened in beauty. Man himself huddled together, pushing and crowding others in far too great a number.

'A world from which solitude is extirpated, is a very poor ideal. Solitude in the sense of being often alone, is essential to any depth of meditation or of character; and solitude in the presence of natural beauty and grandeur, is the cradle of thoughts and aspirations which are not only good for the individual, but which society could ill do without.'[45]

While such a view echoed the romantics, praising inspiration and granting economic growth a very low priority, it also made control of population essential. For the good society to be reached at all, population would have to 'bear a gradually diminishing ratio to capital and employment'; responsibility in sexual conduct was just as significant to the future as responsibility in social conduct.

There is nothing in Mill's treatment of *laissez-faire* and socialism, then, which is incompatible with his moral and political philosophy. There are no major contradictions to exploit and no obvious tensions to be considered. On the contrary, both Mill's pragmatism and his eclecticism seem to have been strongly confirmed by his economic thinking. The *Principles* itself was written to conciliate and to produce agreement between competing economic schools. Like the *Logic*, it can be seen as part of a complete rejection of narrow and sectarian dogmas in favour of a broader and more tolerant stance. In his treatment of *laissez-faire* and socialism Mill was always careful to avoid commitment to single ends either for individuals or for society as a whole; nor did he believe it possible to overcome the limitations inherent in particular circumstances. Indeed, political economy was a science of particular cases, and both the *laissez-faire* and the socialist principles were to be assessed by considering the limits of their practical application, not by assuming their truth *a priori*. Mill's notion of future society also tends to confirm the non-dogmatic bent of his thinking. Many futures were possible, and this fact alone was sufficient to recommend a plurality of experiments in the present. If there were no final truths about human nature in politics and no single end to direct all conduct, then belief in one ultimate future was absurd. While Mill himself obviously inclined towards a property owning and co-operative ideal where economic growth had a low priority, the very nature of this ideal and the contemplative mode of living it supposed made detailed blueprints for the future unthinkable. Utopias were for sectarians, for all those convinced by single truths and sufficiently authoritarian to wish to impose them on other people. Like Comte, the sectarian had forgotten that government 'exists for all purposes whatever that are for man's good: and the highest and most important of these purposes is the improvement of man himself as a moral and intelligent being'.[46] In Mill's view, there was no reason why the future should be treated as an exception.

Notes Chapter IV

1 J. Stillinger (ed.), *Autobiography* (London, O.U.P., 1971), p. 132.

2 Mill to d'Eichthal, *The Earlier Letters of John Stuart Mill, 1812–1848* (Toronto, Univ. of Toronto Press, 1963), *Collected Works*, vol. XII, p. 48.

3 The phrase is from S. R. Letwin, *The Pursuit of Certainty* (London, Cambridge Univ. Press, 1965), p. 286. Characteristic misinterpretations of the *laissez-faire* principle can be found in Gertrude Himmelfarb, *On Liberty and Liberalism* (New York, Alfred Knopf, 1974), part IV and in S. S. Wolin, *Politics and Vision* (London, George Allen & Unwin, 1961), part 9. Far more sensible and far more scholarly are Pedro Schwartz, *The New Political Economy of J. S. Mill* (London, Weidenfeld & Nicolson, 1972) and L. Robbins, *The Evolution of Economic Theory* (London, Macmillan & Co., 1970). On Mill's originality as an economist see G. J. Stigler, 'The Nature and Role of Originality in Scientific Progress', *Economica*, vol. XXII, Nov. 1955 and also N. B. de Marchi, 'The Success of Mill's Principles', *History of Political Economy*, vol. 6, no. 2, Summer 1974, pp. 119–57, an article emphasising the eclectic function of the *Principles*.

4 'Coleridge', *Essays on Ethics, Religion and Society* (Toronto, Univ. of Toronto Press, 1969), *Collected Works*, vol. X, p. 156.

5 See for instance, N. Rosenberg, 'Mandeville and Laissez-Faire', *Journal of the History of Ideas*, vol. XXIV, no. 2, April–June 1963, pp. 183–96 and M. Albaum, 'The Moral Defences of the Physiocrats' Laissez-Faire', *Journal of the History of Ideas*, vol. XVI, no. 2, April 1955, pp. 179–97. One interesting exploration of some of these themes is H. B. Acton, 'Distributive Justice, The Invisible Hand and the Cunning of Reason', *Political Studies*, vol. XX, no. 4, Dec. 1972, pp. 421–31.

6 For examples see the collection edited by A. W. Coats, *The Classical Economists and Economic Policy* (London, Methuen & Co., 1971), in particular articles 1, 2, 4 and 7. There is also A. J. Taylor, *Laissez-Faire and State Intervention in Nineteenth-Century Britain* (London, Macmillan & Co., 1972) and H. Scott Gordon, 'Laissez-Faire', *International Encyclopaedia of the Social Sciences* (New York, Macmillan, 1968), vol. VIII, p. 546 ff. Henry Parris handles the problem in the context of the growth of government, see *Constitutional Bureaucracy* (London, George Allen & Unwin, 1969), in particular ch. IX.

7 Mill to Cairnes, *Letters*, op. cit., XVII, p. 1764.

8 'Employment of Children in Manufactories', *Examiner*, 29 January 1832, pp. 67–8.

9 *Autobiography*, op. cit., pp. 115–16.

10 ibid., p. 116.

11 'Municipal Institutions', *Examiner*, 11 August 1833, pp. 496–7.

12 *Autobiography*, op. cit., p. 116.

13 From Tocqueville, 'Voyages en Angleterre', quoted in P. Schwartz, *The New Political Economy of J. S. Mill* (London, Weidenfeld & Nicolson, 1972), ch. 6, p. 111.

14 *A System of Logic* (London, Longmans, 1970), bk VI, ch. XII, sect. 4, p. 618. Mill had emphasised in the previous section that rules of conduct were only provisional: 'they point out the manner in which it will be least perilous to act'. The error of the 'geometrical school' was precisely a belief in unbending, universal principles.

15 *Principles of Political Economy* (Toronto, Univ. of Toronto Press, 1961), *Collected Works*, vol. III, bk V, ch. XI, p. 951. Mill made the usual exceptions of course, lunatics, idiots and infants were not the best judges of their own interests, nor were those of 'immature years and judgement'. In all of these cases, 'the foundation of the *laissez-faire* principle breaks down entirely'.

16 ibid., bk II, ch. VII, sect. 2, p. 280. My quotation follows the ms. and the 1848–9 editions of the *Principles*. The edition does not, however, affect the general point.

17 Mill to d'Eichthal, *Letters*, op. cit., XII, p. 37. Mill went on to point out the disadvantages of placing government in the hands of the principal '*industriels*' and in 'the *savans* and *artistes*'. In England, these were the three 'classes of persons you would pick out as the most remarkable for a narrow and bigoted understanding, and a sordid and contracted disposition as respects all things wider than their business or families'.

18 'Vindication of the French Revolution of February 1848, in Reply to Lord Brougham and Others', *Dissertations and Discussions* (London, Parker & Son, 1859), vol. II, pp. 335–410.

19 The speech is reprinted in *Chapters and Speeches on the Irish Land Question* (London, 1870), pp. 108–25. The speech is dated March 1868; our quotation is p. 118.

20 For more information see 'Explanatory Statement', 'Programme of the Land Tenure Reform Association' (London, 1871), *Dissertations and Discussions*, op. cit., vol. IV and 'Presidential Address to the Land Tenure Reform Association', ibid., IV, pp. 251–65; also IV, pp. 288–302, 'The Right of Property in Land'.

21 Mill to Helps, *Letters*, op. cit., XVII, p. 2002.

22 'Vindication', op. cit., p. 395. Mill is vague about what is entailed by a commitment to equality. He had no time for the egalitarianism associated with Chartism, and in his Diary he distinguished a high-minded from a greedy and grasping passion for equality: 'It is only the high-minded to whom equality is really agreeable. A proof is that they are the only persons who are capable of strong and durable attachments to their equals; while strong and durable attachments to superiors or inferiors are far more common and are possible to

the vulgarest natures' (Diary, Hugh Elliot (ed.), *The Letters of John Stuart Mill* (London, Longmans et al., 1910), vol. II, Appendix A, 29 March, p. 383).

23 See, for instance, Pedro Schwartz, 'J. S. Mill and Socialism', *Mill News Letter*, vol. IV, no. I, Fall 1968, where Schwartz concludes that Mill ought to be considered a 'radical individualist', but not a 'socialist'.

24 *Principles*, op. cit., bk II, ch. I, sect. 4, p. 214.

25 ibid., bk V, ch. XI, sect. 2, p. 938.

26 'Centralization', *Edinburgh Review*, April 1862, p. 345.

27 *Principles*, op. cit., bk V, ch. XI, sect. 2, p. 937. The insertion marked [ ] is mine.

28 ibid., p. 938.

29 'Coleridge', op. cit., p. 156.

30 *Principles*, op. cit., bk II, ch. XIII, sect. 2, p. 372. A short, reliable and eminently sensible guide to Mill's views on population and population control is F. E. Mineka, 'J. S. Mill and Neo-Malthusianism', *Mill News Letter*, vol. VIII, no. I, Fall 1972, pp. 3–10.

31 John Walter III became editor of *The Times* in 1847. He was a devout Puseyite and his attachment to the Oxford Movement was a decisive feature of editorial policy. Mill noticed all of this himself, claiming that *The Times* 'falls in with everything which Puseyism has set going'. Mill to Chapman, *Letters*, op. cit., XIII, p. 641.

32 ibid., p. 640.

33 ibid., p. 641.

34 'The Claims of Labour', *Dissertations and Discussions*, op. cit., vol. II, p. 206.

35 'Constraints of Communism', *Leader*, 3 Aug. 1850, p. 447.

36 'The Claims of Labour', op. cit., pp. 216–17.

37 'Centralization', op. cit., pp. 349–50.

38 'Chapters on Socialism', *Essays on Economics and Society* (Toronto, Univ. of Toronto Press, 1961), *Collected Works*, vol. V, p. 740.

39 *Principles*, op. cit., bk IV, ch. VI, sect. 2, p. 754.

40 'The Negro Question', *Fraser's Magazine*, vol. XLI, Jan.–June 1850, p. 28.

41 'Wordsworth and Byron', E. Alexander (ed.), *John Stuart Mill: Literary Essays* (Indianapolis, Bobbs-Merrill, 1967), Appendix, p. 353.

42 *Principles*, op. cit., bk IV, ch. VI, sect. 2, pp. 754–5.

43 ibid., p. 756.

44 ibid., p. 756.

45 *Principles*, op. cit., bk IV, ch. VI, sect. 2, p. 756.

46 Mill to d'Eichthal, *Letters*, op. cit., XII, p. 36. This letter contains the now famous statement, 'Men do not come into the world to fulfil one single end, and there is no single end which if fulfilled even in the most complete manner would make them happy'.

Chapter V

Liberty and Individuality

Although *On Liberty* was 'carefully composed' and 'sedulously corrected' before publication in 1859, every sentence being read, weighed and criticised time and time again after the completion of the first draft in 1854, readers of the essay have never agreed either on what Mill's argument actually was, or on the relation of that argument to his intellectual history. The essay remains an enigma, puzzling commentators and provoking widely differing reactions. This was just as true of Mill's immediate contemporaries as of more recent commentators. John Morley, for instance, defended the essay against Carlyle, pointing out that the book was 'one of the most aristocratic' ever written. Mill was far too frightened of the unchecked and 'undirected course of democracy' to have ever considered writing anything else. James Fitzjames Stephen, on the other hand, thought that Mill had formed a much too favourable view of human nature. He had obviously become a rather simple-minded optimist; the essay itself was the product of a mere worshipper of variety.[1] And while the anonymous reviewer in *Bentley's Quarterly Review* was bitterly disappointed by Mill's failure to provide any workable principles, Buckle was convinced of the exact opposite: Mill's genius was precisely to have achieved a perfect union of practice and speculation.[2] Quite apart from the content of the essay, there are also difficulties raised by Mill's whole approach to the question of liberty. In the *Autobiography*, for example, Mill described his essay as 'a kind of philosophic text-book of a single truth'; that truth was 'the very simple principle' of self-protection, which was 'entitled to govern absolutely the dealings of society with the individual in the way of compulsion and control'. The very idea of formulating a single, simple and absolute truth is remarkable. Mill's eclecticism, as well as his *laissez-faire* commitment to a plurality of social experiments and political ideas, had always led him to object to the one-sidedness of single principles. Even more remarkable, perhaps, is the summing up offered in the essay. Here, Mill wrote not of one single principle, but of 'two maxims which together form the entire doctrine of this Essay'. With these kinds of consideration in mind, one wonders whether it is possible to find an entirely consistent argument.

Some disagreement is inevitable of course. In fact, Mill had more than one principle, and was concerned with more than one issue when he wrote *On Liberty*. His careful and sedulous corrections failed to remove all of the ambiguities in his argument, while his desire to consecrate the essay to the memory of Harriet Taylor, who died in 1858 at Avignon on the way to Montpellier, meant that no rewriting could be undertaken in the light of contemporary criticism and later reflections. Even so, despite all of these provisos, there are far too many simple misconceptions of the essay, some of which may be cleared up straight away. Commentators still tell us, for instance, that Mill unlike Green or Bosanquet adopted the negative and not the positive notion of liberty as if this were a real and deliberate choice made between competing alternatives.[3] There is no evidence at all that Mill did make such a choice; for whatever reason, the choice was simply not available to him. Another misconception, less common now perhaps than a few years ago, is to suggest that Mill's main concern was with the enforcement of morals. The essay *On Liberty*, so this argument runs, was concerned with the function of the state in moral matters; the primary concern was to specify the relationship between law and morality.[4] Again there is no evidence that this was Mill's main concern, or that he ever considered making it his main concern. Quite properly, both of these misconceptions can be brushed aside. The question is what remains: how should *On Liberty* be interpreted; what was Mill's understanding of liberty and individuality?

It would seem that Mill's main concern was to demonstrate that liberty was consistent not only with the 'imposition of social obligations by law', but also with the 'imposition' of persuasion by opinion and example. In the 1859 essay, the attempt to demonstrate this rested explicitly upon a distinction between two types of rule: those rules applying to the province of virtue, that is to self-regarding behaviour, and those rules applying to the province of duty, that is to other-regarding behaviour. This distinction was first introduced in the introductory part of the essay where Mill defined the 'practical question' 'on which nearly everything remains to be done'. The question was not about the state and morality, nor had it anything to do with negative and positive liberty;[5] rather, it had to do with 'the fitting adjustment between individual independence and social control'. The argument is plain enough. In any society there have to be restraints upon the actions of people. 'Some rules of conduct, therefore, must be imposed, by law in the first place, and by opinion on many things which are not fit subjects for the operation of law.' Both types or kinds of rule, whether of law or of opinion, necessarily involved some degree of restraint upon free agency, but the requirements for each type of rule to operate effectively were quite different. Rules of opinion which operated by advice, instruction and persuasion, required an active and disinterested concern for the character and conduct of other people, even when that character and conduct had occasioned no perceptible harm to any person or persons other than the agent. This argument merely repeats the conclusions of Mill's new or revised utilitarianism: moral judgement was judgement of person as well as of conduct, judgement of character as well as of consequences. These rules, then, were the consequence of active and critical free inquiry and their end or function was to encourage self-culture and to promote self-regarding virtues. Rules of law, on the other hand, like the authoritative interference of government, operated by sanction and prohibition. These rules were to be imposed only when conduct either threatened or actually affected the legitimate rights and interests of a person or persons other than the agent;[6] such rules required evidence of harm in particular cases, and all of these cases had to be considered separately. The prohibitive regulation of behaviour, whether on *a priori* grounds or by deduction from general theories, was completely improper. This argument, in turn, merely repeats the conclusions of Mill's pragmatic commitment to *laissez-faire*: when individual conduct is responsible and when enlightened choices are being made, interference by law is both unnecessary and unjust.

Hence, in Mill's opinion, the liberty of the individual did not entail freedom from persuasions and inducements, but it did suppose these to be different in kind from legal, social and political sanctions. Rules of opinion and rules of law were different types of rule, not only in their areas of application, but also in the means that could be used to attain their end. While rules of law were concerned solely with the other-regarding consequences of action, with actions involving breaches of duty and clear harm to others, rules of opinion were concerned solely with the quality of self-regarding behaviour where no question of harm to others or of duty arose at all. Mill himself emphasised over and over again that his understanding of liberty ruled out selfish indifference. His argument did not pretend 'that human beings have no business with each others' conduct in life, and that they should not concern themselves about the well-doing or well-being of one another, unless their own interest is involved'; on the contrary, 'there is need of a great increase of disinterested exertion to promote the good of others'. Mill insisted, however, that 'disinterested benevolence can find other instruments to persuade people to their good than whips and scourges, either of the literal or the metaphorical sort'.[7] The significance of this is often ignored or overlooked: the choice is not between coercing a person or leaving him alone, the choice is between coercion and persuasion and between the threat of punishment and the appeal of reasonable argument. If persuasion and rational exhortation cannot be distinguished from compulsion and coercion, then there could be no adequate distinction between law and opinion, between duty and virtue and between self-regarding and other-regarding actions. Liberty would simply cease to exist. There would be no criteria by which to distinguish those actions which are mainly the concern of the individual and those in which society had a legitimate interest. Consequently, the practical question of a 'fitting adjustment' between 'individual independence' and 'social control' would never arise at all.

Mill's solution to the problem of individual independence and social control has already been hinted at. If men were free to adopt their own rules of conduct in pursuit of an ideal character, then they were also free to persuade others to adopt them. Were this freedom exercised fully, there would be the likelihood of greater agreement, and less need for recourse to sanction and coercion; the whole ethos of politics would then be less coercive, and fewer rules would need to be imposed on authority.[8] For this reason, *On Liberty* is full of pleas for people to abandon common notions of politeness and to overcome the English reticence at pointing out other people's faults. There should be honest criticism, and a greater concern for others, simply because this would involve an appeal to reason and a lessening of the despotism of custom: a despotism, Mill added, which effectively prevented 'any misgiving respecting the rules of conduct which mankind impose on one another'.[9] In short, the main threats to liberty derived from indifference; the danger was a simple lack of concern, either for oneself or for others. Indifference made persuasion either very difficult or impossible, so maintaining the need for constant recourse to sanction and coercion. This is why, of course, the essay argued that liberty would have no application at all were mankind incapable 'of being improved by free and equal discussion'. To Mill, being free implied a capacity to be educated and to be convinced by good argument. Just as one activity was better than another, if it was preferred by those who were capable of other and different activities, so also choice was freer for those who had 'the capacity of being guided to their own improvement by conviction or persuasion'.[10] This distinction between sanction and persuasion, between coercion and free choice, ultimately between rules of law and rules of opinion, is at the very centre of Mill's understanding of liberty.

To some extent, no doubt, one should view the distinction as an extension of Mill's moral philosophy. Persuasion and sanction differ as virtue and duty differ: the difference is between acts which are meritorious and subject to opinion, and acts which are obligatory and subject to law. Mill spelt out this distinction in several places, most carefully, perhaps, in 'Thornton on Labour and Its Claims', published in the *Fortnightly Review* in 1869.[11] While merit or virtue does concern persons other than the agent, there being an 'innumerable variety of modes in which the acts of human beings are either a cause, or a hindrance, of good to their fellow-creatures', it was still 'for the general interest that they should be left free; being merely encouraged, by praise and honour, to the performance of such beneficial actions as are not sufficiently stimulated by benefits flowing from them to the agent himself'. Duty was in a different category, involving those 'many acts and a still greater number of forbearances, the perpetual practice of which by all is so necessary to the general well-being, that people must be held to it compulsorily, either by law, or by social pressure'. This distinction between 'the province of positive duty and that of virtue' is the basis of the distinction between self and other-regarding actions in *On Liberty*. Although self-regarding faults such as rashness, obstinacy and self-conceit do mainly concern only the person himself, they are, nevertheless, subject to rules of opinion; they can be judged, and people can also act upon their judgements. A person can be called a fool, he can be told that he is a being of an inferior order. One person can 'honestly point out to another that he thinks him in fault' and he has a right to act on his opinion by avoiding the other person's company. And Mill puts one thing beyond doubt: 'In these various modes a person may suffer very severe penalties at the hands of others for faults which directly concern only himself.' This is not punishment, for no one has a duty to be virtuous. The penalties are natural penalties, 'spontaneous consequences of the faults themselves', which are not inflicted to punish but to persuade.[12]

Mill's ideal is obvious perhaps. Ideally, every person would know what other people thought of him; they would also know what he thought of them. Nothing would be hidden or suppressed through doubt, or ignored through indifference. Where rules of opinion operated in such a fashion, the effect would be to make mere feelings, simple likings and dislikings, increasingly irrelevant. Consequently, there would be fewer lapses into intuitionism. Society would tolerate stronger and more diverse judgements, and be much less inclined to accept preferences at face value. Mill was also convinced that inquiry into the character and conduct of others would encourage each person to inquire into the reasons for his own behaviour. In effect, a free society is an active society, full of strong and assertive characters, where everyone is disposed to have reasons for his conduct. The question still remains, however, of the limit to rules of opinion. Granted that persuasion is different from compulsion, how far can persuasion go? Mill's answer is very straightforward. In his view, a person has no right to complain about the penalties attaching to rules of opinion, 'unless he has merited their favour by special excellence in his social relations, and has thus established a title to their good offices, which is not affected by his demerits towards himself'.[13] Much depends on the word 'right' here. Elsewhere in the essay, Mill distinguishes rights by express legal provision and rights by tacit understanding: the latter seems to be the appropriate sense. Mill's point seems to be that if a person can responsibly regulate his other-regarding conduct without being good or excellent in his own character, then he is entitled to conduct his own affairs free from the pressures of opinion. Only if defects of character result in defects of social conduct can a person rightfully suffer 'severe penalties at the hands of others'. If, on the other hand, a person is manifestly able to fulfil his obligations and to perform his duty, then a lack of merit or virtue is acceptable.

The essay *On Liberty*, then, should be taken as a confirmation of Mill's critique of Benthamism. There was no return to psychological hedonism, there was no restitution of mechanical materialism. The essay was also perfectly consistent with Mill's utilitarian ethic of self-development. Liberty did not entail indifference to character: a person's character and conduct was subject to rules and open to persuasion, even where that character and conduct involved no harm to the interests of others, no breach of duty and no interference with other people's rights. A person was entitled to complain about this only if he had demonstrated that his social conduct was 'specially excellent'. Mill would seem to have assumed that self-regarding deficiencies like rashness and obstinacy would manifest themselves in social conduct, though he allowed the possibility of this not being so. Hence, the 'very simple' principle of self-protection, which limited the power of society over individuals to those cases where interference was necessary to prevent harm to others, did not presume it desirable that a person employ his free agency to cultivate standards of conduct and habits of behaviour inappropriate for responsible social conduct. Indifference to character was never a part of Mill's argument. Virtue should be cultivated as well as duty, and one's right to freedom from the pressures of coercion and the persuasions of opinion was contingent upon the uses that liberty was put to. There are no grounds, then, for suggesting that Mill was indifferent or 'neutral' towards self-regarding actions; equally, there is no evidence that he took such actions to be those which affected and concerned the agent alone. The principle of self-protection was invoked to distinguish between persuasion and sanction. As a principle, it limited the power of interference by law to those cases where the rights and interests of persons other than the agent were prejudicially affected; these cases were cases of duty rather than virtue, obligation rather than merit. The one single, absolute and 'very simple' principle turns out to be rather more complex than some commentators have imagined.

Another point should be made. As well as presuming a distinction between virtue and duty and between self-regarding and other-regarding acts, the 'very simple' principle of self-protection also presumed a distinction between conduct which was inappropriate, silly or un-attractive and conduct which was morally wrong. Again, this is often overlooked or ignored. Before he wrote *On Liberty*, Mill had hoped to overcome the pedantic and excessively moralistic character of Bentham-ism by elaborating a prescriptive philosophy of judgement which maintained a distinction between prudential, aesthetic and moral judgements. And no matter the particular variations, this kind of distinction between judgements appeared in almost all of Mill's writings after he had abandoned the two-part theory of morality. In the essay *On Liberty* it is clear that self-regarding conduct, conduct which is subject to rules of opinion, is also conduct to which the words 'moral' and 'immoral' cannot legitimately be applied. According to Mill, self-regarding faults are 'not properly immoralities, and to whatever pitch they may be carried, do not constitute wickedness. They may be proofs of any amount of folly, or want of personal dignity and self-respect; but they are only a subject of moral reprobation when they involve a breach of duty to others, for whose sake the individual is bound to have care for himself'.[14] If this is so, then the word 'moral' cannot be applied to self-regarding virtues. Quite clearly, Mill was limiting moral judge-ments to the other-regarding category; those judgements entailed by the application of rules of opinion were prudential and aesthetic judge-ments, but not judgements about the moral rightness or wrongness of an action. This tends to confirm our interpretation of the essay: Mill was distinguishing persuasion from sanction in terms of a broad distinction between virtue and duty. Virtue was a matter of opinion; duty a matter of obligation and punishment. To designate an action self-regarding was to make moral judgements inapplicable. For Mill, then, the notion of duties to oneself was without meaning; the only sensible interpretation of the phrase was 'self-respect or self-develop-ment, and for none of these is any one accountable to his fellow creatures, because for none of them is it for the good of mankind that he be held accountable to them'.[15]

While there are these pronounced continuities between Mill's moral philosophy and his understanding of liberty, and while it is right to emphasise them, it would be foolish to ignore the fact that the essay itself had a local and specific point of reference. *On Liberty* reveals Mill's continuing concern with national character and his despair at the mediocrity of mass opinion in England. After his breakdown, Mill had built up a fear of social conformity. Some nations were more prone to this than others. Although the small-minded and unimaginative materialism of the English had not prevented the growth of political liberty, it had produced a marked tendency to smugness and intolerance in social relations. More than any other Europeans, perhaps, the English did not welcome departures from customary modes of conduct. They enjoyed doing what others had done before; they were creatures of habit. Like Arnold and Carlyle, Mill took philistinism and habitual conformity to be the main features of the English character. These general and rather diffuse grouses were given particular point in the early fifties by Mill's observations on national politics. The importance of the mass and the relative unimportance of the individual seemed very marked at that time, and the strike of the Amalgamated Society of Engineers in 1852 convinced Mill of the grubby materialism of many members of the working class. All they wanted was high wages and little work, enforced by monopoly powers. Mill was not impressed by the middle classes either: 'I am convinced that any public matter whatever, under the management of the middle classes, would be as grossly, if not more grossly mismanaged than public affairs are now.'[16] In effect, the habit of customary obedience was far more dangerous and far more dispiriting in England than elsewhere because politics were so democratic, the people so materialistic and genuine talent so scarce.

This kind of grumbling pessimism is at the very heart of *On Liberty*. Although Mill denied that he was seeking 'an intellectual aristocracy of *lumières* while the rest of the world remains in darkness',[17] the question how individuality could be protected in England invited pessimism since the despotism of mediocre mass opinion was not only more extensive than political tyranny, but it also left far fewer means of escape. Collective opinion always tended towards a safe and uniform dullness: ideas were fewer in number and narrower in their range. In these circumstances, where the 'opinions of masses of merely average men are everywhere become or becoming the dominant power', perhaps 'the counterpoise and corrective to that tendency would be the more and more pronounced individuality of those who stand on the higher eminences of thought'.[18] As one commentator has remarked, '*On Liberty* was not a defence of the common man's right to live as he liked; it was more nearly an attack on him'.[19] This may be a little unfair. Nevertheless, there are distinct traces of a kind of high-minded disdain for the ordinary man that are reminiscent of Mill's early toryism. *On Liberty* is an essay full of despair and disillusion and this very fact suggests ways in which Mill's arguments about individuality should be approached.

Obviously, if individuality is understood in the Aristotelian sense

JOHN STUART MILL

of autonomy and self-determination and if the main threat to this individuality is the conformity of mass opinion, then individuality has to express itself in questioning common standards and prevailing norms.[20] A person with no inclination to confront these norms, consciously and critically evaluating them, cannot form intentions of his own and cannot be thought an individual. Convention is the enemy, and the common man's conformity to it amounts to a depersonalisation. Unless there was a commitment to call society's standards into question there would be no adequate way of giving meaning to the notion of one's 'own' choice. This does not mean individual choice can only exist by defying norms and conventions. Rather, independent and rational reflection requires an understanding of the possible difference between one's own choices and those of other people; one must be prepared to experience this difference, but not necessarily by continual rejection of common standards. There is some evidence, of course, that Mill thought the majority of people indifferent to individuality in this sense: the majority, at least in England, were quite 'satisfied with the ways of mankind as they now are' and 'cannot comprehend why those ways should not be good enough for everybody'.[21] This explains Mill's statement that the majority do not desire liberty. It is not that they wish to be coerced; they are not choosing to be restrained. It is, quite simply, that they have no choices of their own; they are 'generally without either opinions or feelings of home growth, or properly their own'.[22] And if liberty is lost by a lack of self-determination, then the majority are unfree. On this definition of individuality, only the minority seem capable of autonomy and self-determination; the rest seem content with an undemanding and dull mediocrity.

If, on the other hand, individuality is less to do with choices made in opposition to social norms than with choices each person makes about his own character and his own motives, then to be individual is to be a person of good character actively committed to self-culture. The origins of this idea of individuality in Mill's mental crisis have already been explained. His rejection of 'Philosophic Necessity' and all other related forms of determinist materialism had made room for the romantic ideal of self-development, and opened him to the influence of Wordsworth and Coleridge in the fashioning of a new utilitarian ethic of self-improvement. But 1854, the year in which Mill completed the writing of On Liberty, was also the year in which von Humboldt's The Sphere and Duties of Government was first published in English.[23] On Humboldt's notion of individuality, the end of man was simply the highest and most harmonious development of capacities. An individual was unique, being unlike other people only to the extent that he had developed his own nature for its own sake. This is precisely what Mill

122

himself understood by character: 'A person whose desires and impulses are his own—are the expression of his own nature, as it has been developed and modified by his own culture—is said to have a character.'[24] The ideals specified by this notion of character are fairly clear. To be individual, a person should be energetic and active. Strong impulses led to a greater capacity for good, while strong feelings also 'generated the most passionate love of virtue, and the sternest self-control'. In fact, strong passions governed by a strong will were the clearest marks of an ideally cultivated individual. Here again, it would seem to follow that only a minority were capable of true individuality.

In a third and final sense of individuality, however, there could be no limitation which excluded the majority. In the special sense of privacy, individuality was the right of all. In Mill's view, there was an area or aspect of life within which the individual could pursue his own good in his own way, subject only to rules of opinion and to the persuasions of rational argument. Usually he took this right of privacy to be co-extensive with liberty of conscience, with liberty of thought and with freedom of opinion and sentiment. But, obviously, the notion of a right to private existence made a manifesto or catalogue of privacy unthinkable; each individual was sole judge of his own interest. The right to privacy included everything the individual desired 'subject to such consequences as may follow: without impediment from our fellow-creatures, so long as what we do does not harm them, even though they should think our conduct foolish, perverse, or wrong'.[25] As we have seen, Mill hoped this individuality would not be used to develop traits or habits inappropriate for responsible social conduct: he was not prepared to grant an equal value to all varieties of self-regarding conduct. Even so, there was never any question of abrogating the right of privacy—*On Liberty* may well be ambiguous, but that at least is perfectly clear. The principle of self-protection ruled out interference either for an individual's moral good, or because he would be happier, wiser or better not doing what he had chosen to do. All that Mill insisted upon were the alternatives to coercion and compulsion. Where there was no case for interference by law or sanction, there might still be a case for remonstrating, entreating and arguing with an individual. This is why Mill was bound to conclude the essay with two maxims rather than a single principle. The first maxim was that other-regarding conduct 'may be subjected either to social or to legal punishment, if society is of opinion that the one or the other is requisite for its protection'. The second maxim concerned self-regarding conduct and the right of privacy. Here, compulsion was always unjust and 'advice, instruction, persuasion and avoidance by other people' was all that was acceptable 'if thought necessary by them for their own good'.[26] Liberty was consistent not only with the imposition of social obligations by law, but also with the imposition of persuasion by opinion and example; that was the whole point of Mill's essay.

Some confusion has been caused by Mill's use of the word 'rules' to apply to opinion as well as to law; one commentator has even suggested that Mill believed 'individual rectitude was to be maintained through the coercive use of social norms'.[27] This is a serious misunderstanding. To specify a matter as subject to rules of opinion was, *ipso facto*, to rule out coercion. In talking of rules of opinion, Mill was referring to those rational arguments about conduct where no question of moral right and wrong was involved and, consequently, where no question of reward or punishment was entailed. The paradigm case for rules of opinion was simply one person honestly attempting to persuade another to his point of view. In other writings, Mill made it very clear that rules of opinion were rules or laws only by analogy.[28] For Mill, to talk of a coercive use of opinion was a contradiction in terms. If a matter was indeed a matter of opinion, then no question of force, sanction or coercion could properly arise; on the contrary, the matter was one in which each individual had a right to privacy, subject to other individuals having the right to express their opinions on that conduct.

We are now in a position to relate Mill's understanding of liberty more carefully to his moral and political philosophy.[29] Obviously, Mill's commitment to utility was neither formal nor trivial. The utilitarian distinction between virtue and duty, as well as the distinction between prudential, aesthetic and moral judgements, appears in the primary distinction between self-regarding and other-regarding conduct: the first is the province of virtue, the second the province of duty. While Mill emphasised the need for variety in the first province or category, his own pessimism about national character and a certain high-minded disdain for the ordinary man inclined him to the view that individuality in the sense of self-determination and self-development would be mainly confined to a minority; in the sense of privacy no such limitation applied. We do not, of course, know how large or small Mill thought that self-determining minority would be. There are also strong echoes of Mill's early emphasis on consensus. The other-regarding category, being a category of duty, is an area of life and conduct where agreement is indispensable. The rules of conduct which apply to this province or category are not dependent upon the free agency of individuals; they are rules of law embodying those minimum conditions and necessary forbearances without which a society would not exist at all. Whatever an individual does or is encouraged to do beyond these rules neither affects their obligatory character, nor alters the need for them. The rules of law of the essay *On Liberty* are simply

formal statements of those 'requisites of stable political union' which
Mill had put together in the *Logic*, in the essay on 'Coleridge' and in the
final chapter of *Utilitarianism* under the heading of justice. To emphasise his ideas on self-culture and on the autonomy of the self-
developed individual should not be allowed to obscure this notion of
a rule.

It is very clear what Mill's position was on this matter. There are
rules of conduct, about killing, about the use of force and about stealing,
for instance, which no member of a community has a right to avoid.
The essence of all of these rules is a notion of wrong-doing which is
absolute and which presumes that a person or persons can be rightfully
compelled to perform duties. For Mill, this was the crucial difference
between moral rules and other kinds of rules; and in his view a person
was no less free if, after following these moral rules, that person was
then subject to other rules, rules of opinion, because people disapproved
of his self-regarding conduct on prudential and aesthetic grounds. If
the activities of self-culture did encourage strong feelings and strong
commitments, then a concern for the character and conduct of others
was not only desirable in itself, but also very likely to be unavoidable.
In a society full of strong and varied opinions, the choice could never be
between interference by law and doing nothing: there were certain to be
opportunities for persuasion and inducement involved in 'face to face'
contact between strong characters. Indeed, the whole argument of
On Liberty rested upon the fact that society had means other than
sanctions to bring 'its weaker members up to its ordinary standard of
rational conduct'.[30] Mill had established the importance of this fact in
his examination of the *laissez-faire* and socialist principles. For all of
these reasons, then, *On Liberty* seems to be consistent with his critique
of Benthamism, with his attachment to the romantic ideal of self-
culture and with the main themes of his economic thinking.

Notes Chapter V

1 John Morley, 'Mr. Mill's Doctrine of Liberty', *Nineteenth-Century Essays*
(London, Univ. of Chicago Press, 1970), p. 118. James Fitzjames Stephen,
Liberty, Equality, Fraternity, extract reprinted in Peter Radcliff (ed.), *Limits
of Liberty: Studies of Mill's On Liberty* (Belmont, Wadsworth & Co., 1966),
p. 49.
2 See J. C. Rees, *Mill and His Early Critics* (Leicester, Univ. College, 1956),
pp. 4–5, and Grant Allen (ed.), *The Miscellaneous and Posthumous Works of
H. T. Buckle* (London, Longmans, 1885), vol. 1, p. 75 ff.
3 See for example, G. H. Sabine, *A History of Political Theory* (New York,

Holt, Rinehart and Winston, 1961), ch. XXXII, 'Liberalism Modernized', pp. 701–21.

4 The most obvious example of this kind of interpretation is Patrick Devlin, *The Enforcement of Morals* (London, O.U.P., 1965). A very able criticism of Devlin's whole approach can be found in Alan Ryan, *The Philosophy of John Stuart Mill* (London, Macmillan & Co., 1970), pp. 245–55.

5 *Utilitarianism, Liberty and Representative Government* (London, J. M. Dent, 1966), *On Liberty*, ch. I, Introductory, pp. 68–9.

6 J. C. Rees has made it clear that one needs to consider rights and interests as part of Mill's distinction between self- and other-regarding conduct. See, for instance, Rees, 'A Re-reading of Mill on Liberty', *Political Studies*, vol. 8, 1960, pp. 113–29. Several criticisms of Rees can be found in R. J. Halliday, 'Some Recent Interpretations of John Stuart Mill', *Philosophy*, Jan. 1968, vol. XLIII, no. 163, pp. 1–17. To use the word 'rules' with respect to the exchange and dissemination of opinions is an odd way of talking. Rules of conduct based on rational opinion and honest conviction would seem to be a more accurate reading of the essay. Obviously, there are no 'rules of opinion' as such. A more careful explanation of Mill's meaning is attempted below.

7 *On Liberty*, op. cit., p. 132. Mill continued, 'I am the last person to undervalue the self-regarding virtues; they are only second in importance, if even second, to the social. It is equally the business of eduction to cultivate both'. This whole passage is reminiscent of the debating speech on Wordsworth.

8 There is an attempt to spell out some of the implications of this argument in R. J. Halliday, 'John Stuart Mill's Idea of Politics', *Political Studies*, vol. XVIII, no. 4, 1970, pp. 461–77. For a very different approach, see Richard Wollheim, 'John Stuart Mill and the Limits of State Action', *Social Research*, Spring 1973, pp. 1–30.

9 *On Liberty*, op. cit., Introductory, p. 69.

10 ibid., p. 73. Until this was the case, there was nothing for mankind 'but implicit obedience to an Akbar or a Charlemagne if they are so fortunate as to find one' (Toronto, Univ. of Toronto Press, 1961), *On Liberty*?

11 *Essays on Economics and Society* (Toronto, Univ. of Toronto Press, 1961), *Collected Works*, vol. v, pp. 633–88. See in particular pp. 650–2, where Mill attacks Thornton's *a priori* system of moral duty. All of our quotations are from these pages.

12 *On Liberty*, op. cit., ch. IV, p. 134.

13 ibid., pp. 134–5. On the question of Mill's notion of rights, see J. C. Rees, 'Postscript to "A Re-reading of Mill on Liberty" ', in P. Radcliff (ed.), *Limits of Liberty*, op. cit., pp. 106–7.

14 *On Liberty*, op. cit., ch. IV, p. 135. At the same time, Mill is prepared to talk of immoral dispositions. On the same page, he lists several vices of disposition, such as malice and envy, which 'constitute a bad and odious moral character'.

15 ibid., p. 135. A lively defence of Mill's position on duties can be found in M. G. Singer, *Generalization in Ethics* (New York, Alfred Knopf, 1961), pp. 311–18.

16 Mill to Wentworth Holworthy, *The Earlier Letters of John Stuart Mill, 1812–1848* (Toronto, Univ. of Toronto Press, 1963), *Collected Works*, vol. XIV,

p. 495. On Mill's reaction to the 1852 strike see Schwartz, *The New Political Economy of J. S. Mill* (London, Weidenfeld & Nicolson, 1972), ch. v, 'Trade Unions'.

17 Mill to Alexander Bain, *Letters*, op. cit., xv, p. 631. Mill continued, 'the effect I aim at by the book is, on the contrary, to make the many more accessible to all truth by making them more open minded'.

18 *On Liberty*, op. cit., ch. III, p. 124.

19 S. R. Letwin, *The Pursuit of Certainty* (London, Cambridge Univ. Press, 1965), p. 301.

20 On this and other notions of individuality see Steven Lukes, *Individualism* (Oxford, Basil Blackwell, 1973), part 2 in particular, and A. D. Lindsay, 'Individualism', *Encyclopaedia of the Social Sciences* (New York, 1930–3), vol. VII, pp. 674–80.

21 *On Liberty*, op. cit., ch. III, p. 115.

22 ibid., p. 119.

23 Humboldt's essay had been written when he was a young man in 1791–2 and was first published complete in German in 1852. It is now readily available, of course, as J. W. Burrow (ed.), *The Limits of State Action* (Cambridge, Univ. Press, 1969). The edition also has a useful introduction.

24 *On Liberty*, op. cit., ch. III, p. 118.

25 ibid., Introductory, p. 75. Mill made it clear that the liberties derived from the principle of privacy, liberty of conscience, liberty of tastes and pursuits and liberty of combination, were the defining characteristics of a free society 'whatever may be its form of government'. In this sense, obviously, privacy is also a condition for individuality.

26 ibid., ch. v, p. 149.

27 We are referring to Graeme Duncan, *Marx and Mill* (Cambridge, Univ. Press, 1973), in particular p. 255. Duncan does not distinguish between the opinions imposed by an ascendant class, which Mill always opposed, and the opinions adopted as a result of rational conviction, which Mill always supported; and although he occasionally pretends otherwise, Duncan follows Cowling in presenting Mill as an authoritarian preacher of the virtues of consensus. For a more considered response see J. C. Rees, 'The Reaction to Cowling on Mill', *Mill News Letter*, vol. I, no. 2, pp. 2–11.

28 See, for instance, 'Austin on Jurisprudence', which first appeared in the *Edinburgh Review*, Oct. 1863, reprinted in *Dissertations and Discussions* (London, Parker & Son, 1867), vol. III, pp. 206–74.

29 A substantially different interpretation from my own can be found in D. G. Brown, 'Mill on Liberty and Morality', *Philosophical Review*, April 1972, vol. 81, pp. 133–58.

30 *On Liberty*, op. cit., ch. IV, p. 139.

Chapter VI

Government Bureaucracy and Voting

If Mill's understanding of liberty reflects deep disquiet at the nature of English society, particularly about a tendency to uniformity of opinion and belief, his writings on the selection and organisation of government indicate equally deep worries about the mediocrity of politicians and the incompetence of the ordinary representative. In fact, his whole analysis of the institutions and personnel of government pointed to a paradox. Participation in politics and taking part in decision making was essential to the practical education of a people; the *laissez-faire* principle rested upon the truth of that proposition. But the political process itself was dominated by narrow and merely sectional interests. While the advent of democracy and the growth of popularly elected assemblies made increased participation inevitable, it also increased the scope for incompetence and for the exercise of rather mundane talents in pursuit of doubtful ends. Mill was very well aware of this paradox. Democracy was a mixed blessing, and he was always prone to a kind of grumbling pessimism about popular government for this reason. He was also unusually quick to spot imperfections and to be overwhelmed by the sordid and prosaic quality of political life; at best he was a reluctant democrat, constantly shaking his head in disapproval. The high-minded toryism of his early reaction against Benthamism was partly responsible. That had generated an irritable and aristocratic disdain for the talents of the ordinary man; a disdain constantly provoked by gloomy observations on national politics and national attitudes. There had been the Engineers' strike in 1852, for instance, which convinced Mill of the depth of working-class intolerance.[1] Polite society, on the other hand, had supported Governor Eyre's barbaric conduct in dealing with a negro rebellion in Jamaica.[2] There had also been a good deal of sympathy among 'the upper and middle classes', even among 'those who passed for liberals', for the pro-slavery cause in America,[3] yet the 1848 revolutions had provoked little but disgust, fear and contempt. All of these events confirmed Mill's early prejudices. The English remained a depressing people, almost completely devoid of ideals and very slow to change.

A large part of the difficulty had to do with the attitudes of those classes traditionally accorded a role in government and a place in public administration. In Mill's view, the ascendant class or classes determined the ethos of a society and set the tone of national character.[4] In England, the middle classes were small-minded, selfish and incompetent. They had no ideals outside of trade, business and the family, and their activities kept up an aggressive and competitive spirit of acquisition. The aristocracy, on the other hand, were lazy and corrupt; they perpetuated an archaic habit of obedience and a blatantly paternalist system of authority. Moreover, as Mill once remarked in the House of Commons, like all stupid people they were generally conservative. These stereotypes about class and class attitudes appeared immediately after the crisis and were to remain a permanent part of Mill's thinking. The upper and middle classes were always a great disappointment to him. So while he looked forward to the end of the old ascendancy of wealth and privilege and was usually to be found on the reform side after his commitment to the movement party, it was never with a great deal of confidence. The English always failed to inspire him. This is why so many of his major works, most noticeably *On Liberty* and the essay on *Representative Government*, have the quality of cautionary tales. Both of these essays were shot through with pessimism; they were intended to serve as stern warnings for the future, whether the danger was too great a uniformity of opinion or the threat of incompetent politicians and selfish interests.

To a limited extent, perhaps, Mill was encouraged by the attitudes of the working class. This was particularly so in the thirties and forties. The revolution of 1830 in France, as well as the growth of co-operative associations amongst wage earners in England, held great promise for the future. Social and educational reform would also achieve a great deal. As late as 1872, Mill felt able to inform Auberon Herbert that the working class 'less than any other class, turn away contemptuously from the supposition that life may be inspired by other objects than self-interest in the lower sense of the term'.[5] All in all, however, the encouragement was occasional and rather flimsy. Mill never quite lost a considered aversion for the working class and a somewhat patrician disdain for its interests. The working class still pursued 'their political and economic objects from class selfishness instead of disinterested principle'. They still wanted far too much money for too little work. They were also too exclusive and too sectional in their unions and associations, showing all of the signs of sectarianism. As a candidate for the Westminster constituency, Mill was quite happy to repeat his belief that although they were ashamed of being so, the English working classes were 'generally liars'; a belief he had first expressed in 1859 as part of an argument against the secret ballot in his pamphlet 'Thoughts on Parliamentary Reform'. This kind of high-minded yet gloomy pessimism helps to account for two of the most distinctive features of Mill's political thinking: his cautious pragmatism which earnestly sought to avoid extremes, and his persistent desire for special expertise, whether expressed in the general form of a clerisy or in the particular voice of those instructed in science. If the first made Mill timid about the progress of democracy and about too rapid an extension of the franchise, the second gave him decided views on the need for experts in legislation and administration. This mixture of timidity and pessimism with great confidence in experts and professionals is crucial to the make up of Mill's political thinking. It is our main concern in this chapter.

The pessimism is clearest, possibly, in Mill's analysis of interest. He adopted a psychological or naturalistic notion of interest rather than a normative one. A person had an interest in X when he wanted X. Consequently, 'everybody has as many different interests as he has feelings; likings or dislikings, either of a selfish or a better kind'.[6] To be caused pain or loss was to suffer damage to one's interests. This association of interest with feeling made two other plausible notions of interest irrelevant. The notion of a 'real' or 'best' interest to which actions should conform was a simple redundancy, while the standpoint of an unprejudiced observer capable of assessing 'legitimate' interest was completely inadmissible. For Mill, to state that X is an interest for A is only to state that A presently wants or desires X. Although he distinguished between 'immediate and direct' interests and 'indirect and remote' interests, in other words between immediate want satisfaction and those interests which put the agent in a better position to satisfy his wants in the future, there was no doubt in his view which kind of want would be pursued. Human beings would pursue 'almost exclusively those which are obvious at first sight, and which operate on their present condition'. In effect, one had to conclude that people would 'follow their own selfish inclinations and short-sighted notions of their own good, in opposition to justice, at the expense of all other classes and of posterity'.[7] There would be no disinterested regard for others; sacrifices would be made only rarely. 'It cannot be maintained that any form of government would be rational which required as a condition that these exalted principles of action should be the guiding and master motives in the conduct of average human beings.'[8] This is either deep pessimism or uncompromising realism. And the harshness of the judgement was confirmed by Mill's observations on the nature of class antagonisms. The interests of those who bought labour were certain to be opposed to the interests of those who sold labour. Each group or class had a perception of its own class position and would endeavour to use politics to further its interests against those of the other class. In politics, class was certain to be both selfish and divisive.[9]

It is hardly surprising, then, that in all of his major writings on government and Parliament, after the essay on 'Bentham' in 1838, Mill should identify the danger of 'class legislation' as one of the constant threats to good government. Indeed, in the essay on *Representative Government* at least, he seems to have no answer to the problem. He speculated about the possibility of each class balancing the other, influencing roughly the same number of votes in Parliament and so leaving the initiative to the minority who valued 'reason, justice and the good of the whole'. In the end, however, his fear of class legislation seems to have been overcome only by denying the reality of class and by pretending that interest is something other than immediate want satisfaction. According to Mill, the reason why 'justice and the general interest mostly in the end carry their point' is that 'the separate and selfish interests of mankind are almost always divided'. In some cases as well, private interest coincides with what is objectively right. There are also those who are governed 'by higher considerations'. In a representative system of government, Mill reminded his readers, interests would always need to carry 'those who act on higher motives' and with 'more comprehensive and distant views'.[10] One hardly needs to point out the contradictions. By his own definition, a class is not divided and its interests are not separated. And if by interest we mean immediate want satisfaction, then there can be no question of acting upon 'higher considerations': all wants are equally justifiable. Mill's own language in the essay indicates the truth of the matter. These were pious hopes; the section on the 'infirmities and dangers' of representative government was written more to give warning of the problem than to suggest a final solution. The answer to the problem of sectional interest and class legislation has to be found elsewhere, in his views on bureaucracy and voting.

Confidence in the special expertise of the professional administrator appeared in Mill's thinking almost immediately after the crisis of 1826. The origins of this confidence are obscure. It may have arisen from Mill's admiration for Prussia and for the efficiency of the Prussian civil service. Possibly it was sustained by contacts with the Saint-Simonians and the Coleridgeans, since both schools were fond of emphasising the need for a group or class of decision makers with superior knowledge. The aristocratic principle of special excellence provided by inspired leadership and sound administration had also been an integral part of

Mill's ideal toryism. Like all of the romantics, Mill was inclined to ease his fears about the advent of democracy with thoughts of a new and unparalleled intellectual ascendancy; and each extension of the franchise, however modest in scope, only served to illustrate the importance of the independent and intelligent administrator. The new pattern of central administration which emerged after 1830 was valuable because it produced just those skills which popular government could rely upon. But whether these were decisive considerations or not, the simple fact remains that for thirty-five years Mill worked at India House in a non-representative system of government run by bureaucrats, first as a clerk and then as Chief Examiner of Correspondence which was the position his father had occupied.[11] Bureaucracy was a part of his daily routine and the work of the East India Company was a living example of just how much the dedicated professional could achieve.

In the case of the East India Company, Mill was absolutely convinced that an independent and professional bureaucracy had established progressive government to the benefit of the Indians. In his evidence to the Select Committee on the East India Company's Charter in 1852, he argued the now familiar case.[12] A professional administrative class was relatively free from patronage, clientage and corruption. Unlike the politician, the good bureaucrat could be independent in the face of sinister interests and sordid connections; he was better placed to show his responsibility to society and his attachment to the public good. For instance, those who were sent out as candidates to the home government of India 'were generally unconnected with the influential classes in this country, and out of the range of Parliamentary influence. The consequence is, that those who have the disposal of offices in India have little or no motive to put unfit persons into important situations, or to permit unjustifiable acts to be done by them'. In Mill's opinion, this would cease to be the case if changes in the government of India led to contacts with 'the ordinary channels of political or Parliamentary influence'. In replying to the question whether the aristocracy should be excluded from the government of India, Mill confirmed his distaste for sectarianism and his preference for the bureaucrat who stood independent of party. 'I see no reason for excluding anyone; but it does seem to me undesirable that those who are appointed to situations in India should be persons permanently connected with political parties, or with Parliamentary influence at home.'[13]

While one might locate Mill's views as part of a typically 'English' theory of administration, stressing the independence, fairness and all-round abilities of the professional administrator, there was obviously a good deal of special pleading as well. Throughout his employment by the East India Company, Mill hoped the government of India would not be 'placed at the mercy of public ignorance, and the presumptuous vanity of political men'.[14] The sentiment seems patently obvious. In this case, government was a private concern in which public debate had no part. At the same time, however, Mill strongly supported competitive entry into the British Civil Service. Here there was no question of a tutelary relationship between government and the people, and Mill could defend a variety of reform proposals on several grounds. With a competitive entry, patronage would have to be given on merit and not by favour; the benefits of competition would also spread more widely in society. But there is little doubt, even so, that Mill's support for the Northcote–Treveleyan report was conceived in a spirit of disdain for the littleness of party politics and the incompetence of parliamentary procedures. Mill advocated the extension of open competition and examination to America, for instance, precisely to help break down the dominance of career politicians: a good and efficient bureaucracy would clamp down on excesses. If the English system were adopted, 'nearly all the corruption and the larger half of the virulence of mere party conflict' would 'necessarily cease'. Mill was not hopeful, however: the English system would undoubtedly 'encounter the utmost hostility from the professional politicians who are the great perverters of free government'.[15] This hostility to party and to party politics has often been commented on; what remains remarkable is the extent of Mill's disdain. The dedicated and intelligent bureaucrat was not only preferable in those systems of government where there was a tutelary relationship between rulers and people, but also in those societies where there was a representative system of government. The bureaucrat was always preferable to the politician.

This preference for the bureaucrat over the politician was made absolutely clear in the essay on *Representative Government*. Time and time again, Mill pointed to the incompetence of the elected representative, and despite his eulogies of Athenian politics, he produced several arguments to justify curtailing the activities of elected representatives. Most of these arguments are familiar ones. The framing of legislation was a job for experts, requiring better qualifications 'than a fluent tongue and the faculty of getting elected by a constituency'; administration was a skill only capable of being learnt by experience and so best left to professional administrators; popular assemblies were not noted for containing 'a selection of the greatest political minds in the country'. But whatever the particular argument, the conclusion was always the same: the representative assembly should confine itself to watching and controlling the government, publicising its acts and airing a variety of opinions; assemblies should know and acknowledge 'that talking and discussion are their proper business, while *doing*, as the result of discussion, is the task not of a miscellaneous body, but of individuals specially trained to it'.[16] The institutional device Mill favoured was a commission of legislation, 'not exceeding in number the members of a Cabinet', who would prepare and draft legislation for the approval of Parliament. This commission had no power to enact law, nor could it refuse to draft legislation approved in principle by Parliament, but Mill obviously saw the commission as the beginning of a genuine separation of functions. The elected representative would control and criticise: the professional administrator would handle the actual conduct of affairs. In this way, 'the acquired knowledge and practised intelligence of a specially trained and experienced Few' would be secured to the nation and the danger of class legislation would be diminished.[17]

Whether this distinction between the roles of the representative and the bureaucrat should be seen as part of a broader distinction between policy and administration, is a matter of conjecture. Mill did not make it clear how much initiative the legislative commission would have, and the details of the relationship between commission and Parliament are left rather obscure. For instance, Mill clearly envisaged depriving Parliament of the power of amendment, which was a niggling and time-consuming business. Once the commission had drafted a piece of legislation, Parliament had only three choices: the legislation could be passed, rejected, 'or if partially disapproved of', remitted to the commission for reconsideration. How the power of remission differs from the power of amendment is not readily apparent in his own exposition. On the whole, the argument for a legislative commission is best interpreted as part of Mill's general preference for bureaucrats over politicians; quite simply, the professional administrator was more intelligent and technically better equipped for decision making than the elected politician. Mill himself made just this comparison: when comparing 'the intellectual attributes' of a representative democracy with a bureaucracy, he felt bound to conclude in favour of bureaucracy. While it was unfavourable to 'individual energy of mind' and always tended to become 'a pedantocracy', bureaucracy also 'accumulates experience, acquires well-tried and well-considered traditional maxims, and makes provision for appropriate practical knowledge in those who have the actual conduct of affairs'.[18] Although elected representatives and popular assemblies were inevitable and essential, the work of government could only be conducted properly 'by skilled persons bred to it as an intellectual profession'. The politician should stick to discussion and criticism, leaving to the expert as much as was consistent with a representative system. In effect, the elected assembly should 'indicate wants', 'be an organ for popular demands, and a place of adverse discussion for all opinions relating to public matters'. On no account, however, should it pretend to govern; after all, it had more than 'enough to do in providing itself with an amount of mental competency sufficient for its own proper work, that of superintendence and check'.[19]

This concern to limit the role of incompetent representatives and, at the same time, to lessen the dangers of class legislation by securing a more effective representation of minorities, also explains Mill's great enthusiasm for proportional representation and for a system of transferable votes. The particular scheme he favoured was the one advanced by Thomas Hare, a London lawyer and Inspector of Charities, in his book *The Election of Representatives, Parliamentary and Municipal*.[20] The book was first published in 1859 and was an expanded version of a pamphlet stimulated by the reform debates of the fifties and published immediately after the general election of 1857. Mill welcomed the book not so much for its detailed technical suggestions as for its demonstration of how the aristocratic principle could be incorporated legitimately into a representative system. Proportional representation and plural voting would have a truly conservative effect. He begged Cornewall Lewis to read the book, for instance, explaining that he found 'it both a monument of intellect, and of inestimable practical importance at the present moment. His suggestions appear to me the real basis of a reconciliation between Radicalism and Conservatism'.[21] Mill was even more fulsome in his praise when writing to Hare himself. The 'difficulty of popular representation' had been solved for the first time; the author had 'raised up the cloud of gloom and uncertainty which hung over the futurity of representative government and therefore of civilisation'.[22] Mill also promised Hare that he would 'henceforth be a zealous apostle' for the whole scheme, and he was as good as his word. In the article 'Recent Writers on Reform', in the second edition of 'Thoughts on Parliamentary Reform' and in the essay on *Representative Government*, Mill presented Hare's plan as a major advance in political theory and a great step forward in practical politics. Also, as MP for Westminster, Mill formally proposed the Hare plan as an amendment to the Representation of the People Bill in May 1867.

Hare's scheme was far from simple.[23] The total number of votes cast was to be divided by the number of seats contested; the quotient was to be called the 'quota'. Any candidate receiving a number of votes equal to or greater than the 'quota' was to be elected. The voter himself was to be allowed to list as many candidates, in order of preference, as he desired; and, obviously, he could vote for any candidate or candidates in the country. If his candidate of his first choice either came nowhere or else obtained more votes than required by his 'quota', then the elector's vote could be allotted to his second preference and so on. Any candidate who mustered the 'quota' of votes, no matter from how scattered an area, was automatically returned to the House of Commons. The voters whose ballots were assigned to a successful candidate made up the constituency for that member. Consequently, in Hare's plan, the voters had to sign their ballots. In this way, Members of Parliament would be able to identify their constituents and the voters themselves would know who was representing them. Mill himself wanted some minor modifications of the plan. He tended to favour reducing the number of transferable preferences a voter could express; he also wanted devices to prevent voters 'hanging back from the poll'. But, ignoring these minor details, Mill's justification for the scheme was the same as the one offered by Hare himself. Without proportional representation and transferable votes, there would be representation of the numerical majority but not representation of all. In short, the scheme was designed to prevent a working-class majority in Parliament, or, at the very least, to counteract the principle of numerical majorities which was likely to make the working class the predominant influence. While Mill was convinced of other advantages, such as a better quality of candidate and a closer relationship between representative and constituent, the scheme was primarily to stop 'the principal power' being placed 'in the hands of classes more and more below the highest level of instruction in the community'. As one commentator has observed, some of Mill's utterances 'smack of trying to ride the chariot of reform only to apply the brakes'.[24]

Similar concerns inspired Mill's arguments on universal suffrage and plural voting. He was prepared to accept universal suffrage as essential to the education of a people. In the essay on *Representative Government*, he quoted Tocqueville's analysis of American society in support of his case, concluding that 'no arrangement of the suffrage' could be 'permanently satisfactory in which any person or class is peremptorily excluded; in which the electoral privilege is not open to all persons of full age who desire to obtain it'.[25] Yet the temporary exceptions he insisted upon seem to be directed against the poorer sections of the working class, those sections, presumably, whose relative economic deprivation made the need for education and enlightenment even greater than usual. Indeed, throughout the whole argument of *Representative Government*, very little remains of Mill's stated commitment to equality. All those in receipt of parish relief, for instance, should be immediately disqualified from voting. 'He who cannot by his labour suffice for his own support has no claim to the privilege of helping himself to the money of others.'[26] The suffrage should also be restricted to those paying taxes; and since indirect taxes on purchases were 'hardly felt' and were paid by virtually everyone, Mill was inclined to support the introduction of a poll tax or even to require a small annual payment from each registered elector. Mill hardly needs us to apologise for him. His commitment to equality was always vague and insubstantial. The least one can say is that he was consistent: he had never argued for the suffrage as a natural or inalienable right. He was quick to inform Herbert Spencer, for instance, that the doctrine of suffrage as a right and not a trust 'would be enough to corrupt and destroy the purest democracy conceivable. There will never be honest or self-restraining government unless each individual participant feels himself a trustee for all his fellow citizens and for posterity. Certainly no Athenian voter thought otherwise'.[27]

However, Mill was much less interested in commenting on exclusion from the franchise, than in establishing the case for plural voting. Although 'every one ought to have a voice' in public affairs, 'that every one should have an equal voice is a totally different proposition'.[28] This proposition ran counter to 'the natural order of human life' which always accorded the wiser or better man a superior weight. In Mill's view, it was a matter of common sense that the contribution of the intelligent and educated was worth more than that of the ignorant and illiterate. Everyone 'has a right to feel insulted by being made a nobody, and stamped as of no account at all'. However, no one but a fool, 'and only a fool of a peculiar description, feels offended by the acknowledgement that there are others whose opinion, and even whose wish, is entitled to a greater amount of consideration than his'.[29] The conclusion was obvious: those whose opinion was entitled to a greater amount of consideration should be given more votes. Mill was also certain that if the choice was between 'equal universal suffrage' and plural voting, then anyone with doubts about the gallop towards full manhood suffrage 'cannot too soon begin to reconcile himself' to some scheme of plural voting. The problem was not in the choice as such, but in the mechanics of plural voting. How was entitlement to extra votes to be decided? What was the number of votes appropriate to those whose opinions were entitled to greater consideration?

No one should pretend that Mill had very satisfactory answers to these questions. Although education had a better claim to govern than property, Mill saw that there were still a great many practical difficulties. He admitted himself that there was no adequate way of measuring 'individual mental superiority' in the absence of 'such a thing as a really national education or a trustworthy system of general examination', and he recognised that although plural voting was practised in vestry elections and in those of poor law guardians, 'it is not likely to be soon or willingly adopted'. He did toy with the idea of using occupation as a test of intelligence. In the essay on *Representative Government*, he stated his belief that an 'employer of labour is on the average more intelligent than a labourer', a skilled more intelligent than an unskilled man and a 'banker, merchant, or manufacturer is likely to be more intelligent than a tradesman'.[30] Quite rightly, perhaps, he was half-hearted about these and similar occupational tests. A national system of education was what was really wanted; it would then be possible to have the actual achievements of every person certified by public examination. But no matter the doubts about practicality, Mill was convinced that some system of plural voting was necessary to counteract universal suffrage and to prevent the despotism of the numerical majority. Each successive extension of the suffrage reawakened his fears that Parliament would become dominated by working-class representatives. The extent of his fear and his own sense of desperation can be gauged from his correspondence with Thomas Hare and Henry Fawcett. Plural voting and proportional representation offered the only real chance of preventing despotism. 'It is an uphill race, and a race against time, for if the American form of Democracy overtakes us first, the majority will no more relax their despotism than a single despot would.' Mill's sense of desperation was obviously increased by the attitude of Disraeli and the Tories, who did not support the representation of minorities. Once again, 'as it has been through all my lifetime', the radicals would have 'to do duty as Conservatives, often in opposition to those they were attempting to save'.[31]

All of these arguments about proportional representation, about plural voting and about the legislative commission, illustrate the paradox at the centre of Mill's political thinking. He was by inclination an aristocrat, wedded to sound government and bureaucratic expertise. He had no enthusiasm at all for popular assemblies elected by numerical majorities, and was constantly haunted by the fear of a working-class despotism. Yet he also recognised the educative role of political participation: without active and intelligent citizens, all governments, whether representative or not, degenerated into officious paternalisms. Rational men became like children and the opportunities for participation became smaller and smaller; politics simply ceased to be an art and became, instead, an exercise in habitual obedience. Consequently, Mill was forced to conclude in favour of extending the suffrage and of increasing the rate of popular access to decision-making bodies. But, in his case, such a conclusion was bound together with a grumbling pessimism and with a high-minded disdain for the day-to-day conduct of politics. His candidature for the Westminster constituency in 1865 was a good illustration of this. He refused both to spend any money and to campaign. He indicated his indifference to both local and party interests, and rather than argue for his opinions, he merely presented his views in a letter to James Beal who was the head of the committee which had asked him to run for election. The ideal seems obvious enough. The man of independent means and independent mind, unattached to party and with no special interest to represent, was preferable to any other. Indeed, it is difficult to avoid the conclusion that, for Mill, the best politician was either an aristocrat or an administrator. As one commentator has remarked, Mill always seemed to be 'trying to preserve a time when politics was an affair between gentlemen, unsullied by the hurly-burly of the hustings and the crass efforts of the have-nots to claim a larger share of the fruits of society'.[32] This captures the spirit, if not the detail, of Mill's views on government and politics.

Notes Chapter VI

1 Mill used this strike as an example of the 'total absence of any large and generous aims' and an 'almost open disregard of all other objects than high wages and little work for their own small body' (*Principles of Political Economy* (Toronto, Univ. of Toronto Press, 1961), *Collected Works*, vol. III, bk v, ch. x, p. 931).

2 There is no very satisfactory study of Mill's activities during the Eyre controversy and the part he played in the Jamaica Committee. Certainly he made himself very unpopular by his vehement condemnation of Eyre, losing his Westminster seat as a consequence of his activities. Some information can be found in Bernard Semmel, *The Governor Eyre Controversy* (London, MacGibbon & Kee, 1962).

3 J. Stillinger (ed.), *Autobiography* (London, O.U.P., 1971), p. 159. English reaction to the Civil War was particularly galling to Mill. He continued: 'I never before felt so keenly how little permanent improvement had reached the minds of our influential classes and of what small value were the liberal opinions they had got into the habit of professing' (ibid., pp. 159–60).

4 'Wherever there is an ascendant class, a large portion of the morality of the country emanates from its class interests, and its feelings of class superiority' (*On Liberty*, in *Utilitarianism, Liberty and Representative Government* (London, J. M. Dent, 1966), p. 70).

5 Mill to Auberon Herbert, *The Earlier Letters of John Stuart Mill, 1812–1848* (Toronto, Univ. of Toronto Press, 1963), *Collected Works*, vol. XVII, p. 1870. Mill also returned to a favourite theme later in the letter, expressing the hope that the working class might 'be shamed out of the exclusive regulations of many of the trades unions by inducing them to aim at the benefit of the entire labouring population instead of their own trade only' (ibid., p. 1871).

6 'Thoughts on Parliamentary Reform', reprinted in G. Himmelfarb (ed.), *Essays on Politics and Culture* (New York, Doubleday, 1962), p. 330.

7 *Representative Government*, op. cit., ch. VI, p. 254. This notion of interest points to a difference between the psychological assumptions Mill made as a political analyst and those he made as a moral philosopher. Obviously, the

analysis of interest in *Representative Government* runs counter to his own distinction between higher and lower pleasures and tends to weaken his critique of psychological hedonism. This difference, and the reasons for it, is worthy of further study.

8 ibid., p. 253.

9 Very little has been written on Mill's notion of class. One exception, written from a familiar standpoint and rather insensitive to the nuances of Mill's thinking, is J. E. Broadbent, 'The Importance of Class in the Political Theory of John Stuart Mill', *Canadian Journal of Political Science*, vol. I, no. 3, 1968, pp. 270–87.

10 *Representative Government*, op. cit., ch. VI, p. 256.

11 Mill was employed in an official or paid capacity at India House between 1823 and 1858. He wrote an immense amount on the government and administrative system of India. The only serious study of Mill and the Indian experience is Alan Ryan, 'Utilitarianism and Bureaucracy', in G. Sutherland (ed.), *Studies in the Growth of Nineteenth-Century Government* (London, Routledge & Kegan Paul, 1972), pp. 33–62.

12 *Reports from Committees: 1852–53*, vol. XXX, session 4, Nov. 1852–Aug. 1853, pp. 300–12.

13 ibid., item 2950, p. 305.

14 *Representative Government*, op. cit., ch. XIV, p. 335. Mill also stated his view that the 'amount of good government' produced by the East India Company was 'truly wonderful'.

15 Mill to an unidentified correspondent, *Letters*, op. cit., XVII, pp. 1572–3.

16 *Representative Government*, op. cit., ch. V, p. 240.

17 ibid., p. 241.

18 ibid., VI, p. 246.

19 ibid., p. 248.

20 For a detailed account of Hare's scheme and Mill's response to it, see P. B. Kern, 'Universal Suffrage Without Democracy: Thomas Hare and J. S. Mill', *Review of Politics*, vol. 34, July 1972, pp. 306–23.

21 Mill to Cornewall Lewis, *Letters*, op. cit., XV, p. 608. Mill also informed Hare that his scheme was 'not at all Tory, though, in the best sense, Conservative, and having also the advantage of being a strict logical corollary from the broadest principles of Democracy' (*Letters*, op. cit., XV, p. 668).

22 Mill to Hare, *Letters*, op. cit., XV, pp. 598–9.

23 Henry Fawcett wrote a shorter and simplified version of the Hare plan. Both Hare and Mill were inclined to recommend this version in preference to the original. As Mill once remarked, 'like many discoverers', Hare 'has much to learn in the art of presenting his discoveries with a view to popular effect' (*Letters*, op. cit., XV, p. 672).

24 John Vincent, *The Formation of the British Liberal Party 1857–68* (Harmondsworth, Penguin Books, 1972), p. 186.

25 *Representative Government*, op. cit., VIII, p. 280. The pamphlet 'Thoughts on Parliamentary Reform', which in some respects served as a first draft of *Representative Government*, made the same point even more forcibly: 'A person who

is excluded from all participation in political business is not a citizen. He has not the feelings of a citizen. To take an active interest in politics is, in modern times, the first thing which elevates the mind to large interests and contemplations.' Every 'adult human being' should then possess 'the electoral suffrage' ('Thoughts on Parliamentary Reform', op. cit., p. 314).

26 *Representative Government*, op. cit., VIII, p. 282.

27 Mill to Herbert Spencer, *Letters*, op. cit., xv, p. 608.

28 *Representative Government*, op. cit., VIII, p. 283.

29 ibid., p. 284.

30 ibid., p. 285.

31 Mill to Henry Fawcett, *Letters*, op. cit., xv, p. 672.

32 P. B. Kern, 'Universal Suffrage Without Democracy', op. cit., p. 322.

Conclusion

Mill was a cautious and uncertain pessimist, with an extraordinarily acute sense of the dangers of first principles and grand theories. He was always likely to retreat into a disenchanted pragmatism and, more often than not, was to be found shaking his head in a mixture of disbelief and disillusion. Partly this was a question of personal morale. The hopes he derived from the English romantics and the French positivists, after the resolution of his nervous breakdown in 1826, proved to be flimsy and insubstantial when confronted with the press of illiterate and intemperate proletarians upon the institutions of national politics. The growth of the English working class as a consciously separate political force filled him with fear; he was convinced that their grubby materialism would finally issue into a despotism. His observation of the aristocracy and middle classes confirmed the worst of his forebodings. It was also partly a question of intention. Mill designed his political theory with few terminal points; he was more interested in conducting a continuous holding operation than in arriving at a particular destination. In this way, each extreme could be resisted as it appeared, and each bitter controversy could be gently encouraged to fade into comfortable agreement. This was the whole point of Mill's eclecticism and his most enduring commitment as a political thinker. Consensus was indeed his basic value.

But his commitment to consensus was not absolute and all-consuming. The agreement Mill so earnestly sought rested upon the self-conscious and critical choices of all those individuals concerned to understand the difficulties of politics and the dilemmas of moral living. Their agreement could neither be bought nor forced; and without the activities of self-culture and all of the convictions arising from those activities, agreement would either be totally spurious or completely intolerant. This was the lesson that Mill had learned at the feet of the romantics. People should think for themselves and try experiments for themselves, constantly seeking a quality of experience that was unique; only in this way could the conduct of human beings approach responsibility. Like all other activities, morals and politics had to be learnt. As a sceptic prone to disenchantment, Mill was inclined to believe that on the whole people learned slowly and rather badly. There is nothing sinister or reprehensible in this belief: Mill still remained committed to free inquiry and to liberty of conscience and pursuits. And he may well have been right in thinking that when improvement comes, it comes only very slowly, emerging piecemeal here and there: the view is as plausible as any other.

Indeed, despite his emphasis on the methods of observation, analysis and induction and his continuing reputation as a philosopher of science, in politics at least, Mill was most impressed by the limitations of time, place and circumstance. He recognised that skills had only a very local application and that knowledge, like experience itself, could never be complete. In his view, the art of judgement could not be separated from the limitations inherent in particular situations; and while politics was not merely the pursuit of whatever appeared from day to day, the practitioner was forced to proceed pragmatically, case by case, issue by issue, with whatever certainty was to hand. This helps to explain the great range and variety of causes to which Mill was able to commit himself. His firm belief was that, in politics, now one theory was right, now another; one was bound to use whatever was to hand at a particular time. Consequently, dogmatism was always his enemy, and his cautious and uncertain pessimism was matched by a determination to keep his mind open. So while Mill was frequently likely to be grumbling, he was also prepared to learn. This is what made him a serious political thinker.

Bibliography

This is not a complete bibliography. Only works cited in the text are listed below, in the editions used there. The *Bibliography of the Published Writings of John Stuart Mill*, edited by MacMinn, Hainds and McCrimmon, records almost everything that Mill wrote between 1822 and January 1873, however small or unimportant. The *Mill News Letter* is publishing a complete bibliography of writings on Mill in each successive issue, beginning with 'Anonymous' and 'A' in vol. 1, no. 1, Fall 1965.

A *J. S. Mill: Editions and Collections*

The Collected Works of John Stuart Mill (London and Toronto, Univ. of Toronto Press and Routledge & Kegan Paul, 1963–).

Alexander, E. (ed.), *John Stuart Mill: Literary Essays* (Indianapolis, Bobbs-Merrill, 1967).

Elliot, H. (ed.), *The Letters of John Stuart Mill* (London, Longmans Green & Co., 1910).

Himmelfarb, G. (ed.), *Essays on Politics and Culture* (New York, Doubleday, 1962).

Mill, J. S., *Dissertations and Discussions* (London, Parker & Son, 1859, 2 vols.; vol. 3, 1867; vol. 4, 1875).

Mill, J. S., *A System of Logic, Ratiocinative and Inductive* (London, Longmans, 1970).

Mill, J. S., *Auguste Comte and Positivism* (Ann Arbor, Univ. of Michigan Press, 1961).

Mill, J. S., *Utilitarianism, Liberty and Representative Government* (London, J. M. Dent, 1960).

Mill, J. S., *An Examination of Sir William Hamilton's Philosophy* (London, Longmans, Green & Co., 1889).

Schneewind, J. B. (ed.), *Mill's Essays on Literature and Society* (New York, Collier-Macmillan, 1965).

Stillinger, Jack (ed.), *Autobiography* (London, O.U.P., 1971).

Stillinger, Jack (ed.), *The Early Draft of John Stuart Mill's Autobiography* (Urbana, Univ. of Illinois Press, 1961).

B *J. S. Mill: Other Writings*

'The Life of Napoleon Buonaparte', *Westminster Review*, April 1828.

'Review of Herschel's Discourse on the Study of Natural Philosophy', *Examiner*, 20 March 1831, pp. 179–80.

'Employment of Children in Manufactories', *Examiner*, 29 Jan. 1832, pp. 67–8.

'Use and Abuse of Political Terms', *Tait's Edinburgh Magazine*, vol. 1, May 1832, pp. 164–72.

'Pledges', *Examiner*, 1 July 1832, pp. 416–17.

'Austin's Lectures on Jurisprudence', *Tait's Edinburgh Magazine*, vol. 11, Dec. 1832, pp. 343–8.

'Writings of Junius Redivivus', *Monthly Repository*, vol. VII, April 1833, pp. 262–70.

'Blakey's History of Moral Science', *Monthly Repository*, vol. VII, Oct. 1833, pp. 661–9.

'Comparison of the Tendencies of French and English Intellect', *Monthly Repository*, vol. VII, Nov. 1833, pp. 800–4.

'Letter from an Englishman to a Frenchman on a recent Apology', *Monthly Repository*, vol. VIII, June 1834, pp. 385–95.

'Mrs. Austin's Translation of M. Cousin's Report on the State of Public Instruction in Prussia', *Monthly Repository*, vol. VIII, July 1834, pp. 502–13.

'The Rationale of Political Representation', *Westminster Review*, vol. XXX, July 1835, pp. 341–71.

'Reorganization of the Reform Party', *Westminster Review*, vol. XXXII, April 1839, pp. 475–508.

'The Negro Question', *Fraser's Magazine*, vol. XLI, Jan.–June 1850, pp. 25–31.

'Constraints of Communism', *Leader*, 3 Aug. 1850, p. 447.

'Centralization', *Edinburgh Review*, vol. CXV, April 1862, pp. 323–58.

C *Works Cited in Text*

Abrams, M. H., *The Mirror and the Lamp: Romantic Theory and the Critical Tradition* (London, O.U.P., 1953).

Alexander, E., *Mathew Arnold and John Stuart Mill* (New York, Columbia Univ. Press, 1965).

Austin, J., *The Province of Jurisprudence Determined* (London, John Murray, 1861).

Allen, G. (ed.), *The Miscellaneous and Posthumous Works of H. T. Buckle* (London, Longmans, 1885).

Borchard, R., *John Stuart Mill, the Man* (London, Watts & Co., 1957).

Brett, R. L. (ed.), *S. T. Coleridge: Writers and their Background* (London, Bell & Sons, 1971).

Britton, K., *John Stuart Mill* (New York, Dover Pub., 1969).

Bruford, W. H., *The German Tradition of Self-Cultivation* (Cambridge, Univ. Press, 1975).

Bulwer, E. L., *England and the English* (Paris, 1834).

Burrow, J. W. (ed.), *The Limits of State Action* (Cambridge, Univ. Press, 1969).

Burston, W. H. (ed.), *James Mill on Education* (Cambridge, Univ. Press, 1969).

Coats, A. W. (ed.), *The Classical Economists and Economic Policy* (London, Methuen & Co., 1971).

Coburn, K. (ed.), *Coleridge, a collection of Critical Essays* (New Jersey, Prentice Hall, 1967).

Coleridge, S. T., *Collected Letters* (Oxford, E. L. Griggs, 1956).

Coleridge, S. T., *Biographia Literaria* (London, J. M. Dent, 1971).

Coleridge, S. T., *The Friend* (London, William Pickering, 1837).

Coleridge, S. T., *Aids to Reflection* (Liverpool, Edward Howell, 1874).

Comte, A., *Système de Politique Positive* (Paris, Saint-Simon, 1824).

Courtney, W. L., *The Life of John Stuart Mill* (London, Scott & Co., 1889).

Cowling, M., *Mill and Liberalism* (Cambridge, Univ. Press, 1963).

Devlin, P., *The Enforcement of Morals* (London, O.U.P., 1965).

Duncan, G., *Marx and Mill* (Cambridge, Univ. Press, 1973).

Fruman, N., *Coleridge, The Damaged Archangel* (London, George Allen & Unwin, 1972).

Hamburger, J., *Intellectuals in Politics: John Stuart Mill and the Philosophic Radicals* (New Haven, Yale Univ. Press, 1965).

Hare, T., *The Election of Representatives, Parliamentary and Municipal* (London, 1865).

Herschel, J. F. W., *A Preliminary Discourse on the Study of Natural Philosophy* (New York, Johnson Reprint Cor., 1966).
Himmelfarb, G., *On Liberty and Liberalism* (New York, Alfred Knopf, 1974).
Hollis, P. (ed.), *Pressure from Without* (London, Edward Arnold, 1974).
House, H., *Coleridge, the Clark Lectures, 1951–52* (London, Rupert Hart-Davis, 1969).
Jackson, R., *An Examination of the Deductive Logic of John Stuart Mill* (London, O.U.P., 1941).
Letwin, S. R., *The Pursuit of Certainty* (Cambridge, Univ. Press, 1965).
Lindley, D., *The Saint-Simonians, Carlyle and Mill* (Ph.D. thesis, Columbia Univ., 1958).
Lukes, S., *Individualism* (Oxford, Basil Blackwell, 1973).
Macaulay, T. B., *Essays, Critical and Miscellaneous* (Boston, Phillips, Sampson & Co., 1856).
Marmontel, J. F., *Memoirs*, tr. B. Patmore (London, Routledge & Kegan Paul, 1930).
Marx, K., *The Poverty of Philosophy* (Moscow, 1956).
McCloskey, H. J., *John Stuart Mill: A Critical Study* (London, Macmillan & Co., 1971).
Mill, J., *Analysis of the Phenomena of the Human Mind* (London, Longmans et al., 1869).
Mineka, F. E., *The Dissidence of Dissent: The Monthly Repository, 1806–1838* (Chapel Hill, Univ. of N. Carolina Press, 1944).
Morley, J., *Nineteenth-Century Essays* (London, Univ. of Chicago Press, 1970).
Morley, J., *Recollections* (London, Macmillan & Co., 1917).
Mueller, I. W., *John Stuart Mill and French Thought* (Urbana, Illinois Univ. Press, 1956).
Orsini, G. N. G., *Coleridge and German Idealism* (Carbondale, Southern Illinois Univ. Press, 1969).
Packe, M. St J., *The Life of John Stuart Mill* (London, Secker & Warburg, 1954).
Pankhurst, R. K., *The Saint-Simonians, Mill and Carlyle* (London, Sidgwick & Jackson, 1957).
Parris, H., *Constitutional Bureaucracy* (London, George Allen & Unwin, 1969).
Peters, R. S. (ed.), *Brett's History of Psychology* (London, George Allen & Unwin, 1953).
Popper, K., *The Logic of Scientific Discovery* (London, Hutchinson, 1959).
Pym, H. N. (ed.), *Memories of Old Friends* (London, Smith & Elder, 1882).
Radcliff, P. (ed.), *Limits of Liberty: Studies of Mill's On Liberty* (Belmont, Wadsworth & Co., 1966).
Randall, J. H., jr, *The Career of Philosophy* (New York, Columbia Univ. Press, 1965).
Rees, J. C., *Mill and His Early Critics* (Leicester, Univ. College, 1956).
Robbins, L., *The Evolution of Economic Theory* (London, Macmillan & Co., 1970).
Robson, J. M., *The Improvement of Mankind* (London, Routledge & Kegan Paul, 1968).
Ryan, A., *The Philosophy of John Stuart Mill* (London, Macmillan & Co., 1970).
Ryan, A., *J. S. Mill* (London, Routledge & Kegan Paul, 1974).
Sabine, G. H., *A History of Political Theory* (New York, Holt, Rinehart & Winston, 1961).
Sanders, C. R., *Coleridge and the Broad Church Movement* (Durham, N. Carolina Press, 1942).

Schneewind, J. B. (ed.), *Mill: A Collection of Critical Essays* (London, Macmillan & Co., 1969).
Schwartz, P., *The New Political Economy of J. S. Mill* (London, Weidenfeld & Nicolson, 1972).
Semmel, B., *The Governor Eyre Controversy* (London, MacGibbon & Kee, 1962).
Singer, M. G., *Generalization in Ethics* (New York, Alfred Knopf, 1961).
Sutherland, G. (ed.), *Studies in the Growth of Nineteenth-Century Government* (London, Routledge & Kegan Paul, 1972).
Taylor, A. J. (ed.), *Laissez-Faire and State Intervention in Nineteenth-Century Britain* (London, Macmillan & Co., 1972).
Turk, C. C. R., *Samuel Taylor Coleridge and John Stuart Mill* (D.Phil. thesis, Univ. of Sussex, 1970).
Vincent, J. R., *The Formation of the British Liberal Party, 1857–1868* (Harmondsworth, Penguin Books, 1972).
Warren, H. C., *A History of the Association Psychology* (London, Constable & Co., 1921).
Weinberg, A., *Theodor Gomperz and John Stuart Mill* (Geneva, Librairie Droz, 1963).
Wellek, R., *Immanuel Kant in England, 1793–1838* (Princeton, Univ. Press, 1931).

D *Articles Cited in Text*

Acton, H. B., 'Distributive Justice, the Invisible Hand and the Cunning of Reason', *Political Studies*, vol. xx, no. 4, Dec. 1972, pp. 421–31.
Albaum, M., 'The Moral Defences of the Physiocrats' Laissez-Faire', *Journal of the History of Ideas*, vol. xvi, no. 2, April 1955, pp. 179–97.
Britton, K., 'J. S. Mill: A Debating Speech on Wordsworth, 1829', *Cambridge Review*, vol. lxxix, March 1958, pp. 418–23.
Brown, D. G., 'Mill on Liberty and Morality', *Philosophical Review*, April 1972, vol. 81, pp. 133–58.
Burns, J. H., 'J. S. Mill and Democracy, 1829–1861', reprinted from *Political Studies* in Schneewind, op. cit., pp. 280–328.
Cumming, R. D., 'Mill's History of His Ideas', *Journal of the History of Ideas*, vol. xxv, no. 2, April–June 1964, pp. 235–56.
Friedman, R. B., 'An Introduction to Mill's Theory of Authority', in Schneewind, op. cit., pp. 379–425.
Scott-Gordon, H., 'Laissez-Faire', *International Encyclopaedia of the Social Sciences*, vol. viii, p. 546 ff.
Hainds, J. R., 'J. S. Mill's Examiner Articles on Art', *Journal of the History of Ideas*, vol. xi, no. 2, 1950, pp. 215–34.
Halliday, R. J., 'Some Recent Interpretations of John Stuart Mill', *Philosophy*, Jan. 1968, vol. xliii, no. 163, pp. 1–17.
Halliday, R. J., 'John Stuart Mill's Idea of Politics', *Political Studies*, vol. xviii, no. 4, 1970, pp. 461–77.
Kern, P. B., 'Universal Suffrage Without Democracy: Thomas Hare and John Stuart Mill', *Review of Politics*, vol. 34, July 1972, pp. 306–23.
Levi, A. W., 'The "Mental Crisis" of John Stuart Mill', *Psychoanalytic Review*, vol. xxxii, 1945, pp. 86–101.
Lindsay, A. D., 'Individualism', *Encyclopaedia of the Social Sciences* (New York, 1930–3), vol. vii, pp. 674–80.

Marchi, N. B. de, 'The Success of Mill's Principles', *History of Political Economy*, vol. 6, no. 2, Summer 1974, pp. 119–57.

Mill, Anna J., 'John Stuart Mill's Visit to Wordsworth, 1831', *Modern Language Review*, vol. XLIV, 1949, pp. 341–50.

Mineka, F. E., 'J. S. Mill and Neo-Malthusianism', *Mill News Letter*, vol. VIII, no. 1, Fall 1972, pp. 3–10.

Pappé, H. O., 'Mill and Tocqueville', *Journal of the History of Ideas*, vol. XXV, no. 2, April–June 1964, pp. 217–34.

Rees, J. C., 'A Re-reading of Mill on Liberty', *Political Studies*, vol. 8, 1960, pp. 113–29.

Rees, J. C., 'Postscript to "A Re-reading of Mill on Liberty" ', in Radcliff, op. cit., pp. 106–7.

Rees, J. C., 'The Reaction to Cowling on Mill', *Mill News Letter*, vol. I, no. 2, pp. 2–11.

Rosenberg, N., 'Mandeville and Laissez-Faire', *Journal of the History of Ideas*, vol. XXIV, no. 2, April–June 1963, pp. 183–96.

Schwartz, P., 'J. S. Mill and Socialism', *Mill News Letter*, vol. IV, no. 1, Fall 1968, pp. 11–15.

Spence, G. W., 'The Psychology behind J. S. Mill's "Proof" ', *Philosophy*, Jan. 1968, vol. XLIII, no. 163, pp. 18–28.

Stigler, G. J., 'The Nature and Role of Originality in Scientific Progress', *Economica*, vol. XXII, 1955, pp. 293–302.

Stillinger, J., 'The Text of J. S. Mill's Autobiography', *Bulletin of the John Rylands Library*, vol. XLIII, 1960, pp. 220–42.

Thomas, W., 'John Stuart Mill and the Uses of Autobiography', *History*, vol. 56, no. 188, 1971, pp. 341–59.

White, R. J., 'John Stuart Mill', *Cambridge Journal*, vol. V, no. 2, 1951, pp. 86–96.

Wollheim, R., 'John Stuart Mill and the Limits of State Action', *Social Research*, Spring 1973, pp. 1–30.

INDEX

Adams, W. B. (pseud. Junius Redivivus) 52
Amalgamated Society of Engineers 121, 128
America: the politics of 71, 133; similarities with England 15; Tocqueville's writings on 79, 97, 136; English response to slavery in 128
Anti-Corn Law League 106
Aristocracy 54, 129
Aristocratic principle of excellence 34, 69, 131, 135
Arnold, Matthew 121
Art, as distinct from science 76–7
Art of life 60, 109, 120
Art of politics 74, 86–7, 89, 143
Associationism 15, 17, 22–4, 46, 56
Austin, John 56, 69, 75
Authority: and the *Logic* 72; and the physical sciences 71, 73–4; the authoritative intervention of government 103–4
Axiomata Media 29, 52, 63–4, 75, 87

Bacon, Sir Francis 52, 78, 79
Bain, A. 87
Bastiat, F. 95
Beal, James 139
Bentham, Jeremy 13, 15, 35, 58, 60, 62, 63, 81, 101; Mill's separation from Benthamite radicals 49–50; his criticism of Benthamite rationalism 45–7, 51–2, 56–62, 81, 82, 119
Bentley's Quarterly Review 114
Birth-control 15, 104–5, 109
Blakey, Robert 30
Bosanquet, B. 115
Bowring, Sir John 50
Brougham, Lord 100
Buckle, H. T. 114
Bulwer, Edward Lytton 51, 86
Byron, Lord 21, 28, 50

Cairnes, J. E. 95
Cambridge Apostles 14

Carlyle, Thomas 16, 21, 29, 35, 49, 50, 57, 108, 109, 114, 121
Centralisation 96–7, 103–4
Chartism 55, 106
Chemistry and the Chemical Method 81
Class 54, 121, 129–30, 131; working class and the suffrage 54, 136–7; materialism of 121, 138; optimism about 129–30
Clerisy 36–7, 88–9
Coleridge, S. T. 14, 15, 18, 21, 22, 36, 44, 50, 59, 64, 75, 76, 77, 83, 95, 104, 122
Communism 106
Comte, Auguste 27, 29, 48, 71, 87, 88, 89, 99, 111
Consensus 15, 30, 87–8, 124–5, 142; amongst the instructed 70–3; and changes in Mill's views 87–8
Corn Laws 54
Croker, John Wilson 38

d'Eichthal, Gustave 26, 27, 30, 71
Democracy 70, 73, 79, 88, 97, 121, 137, 138
De Vigny, Alfred 44
Dialectics 79
Disraeli, Benjamin 138
Durham, Lord John 54, 55
Duty 60, 117–18, 120, 124–5

East India Co. 132; India House 13, 35, 132; Select Committee on 132
Eclecticism 25–6, 29–30, 32–3, 39, 60, 69, 142
Edinburgh Review, The 79, 103, 106
Education: Mill's attitude to own 16–17, 24; Benthamite philosophy of 23, 45–6; and the clerisy 36–7; and the feelings 28–9, 32, 46–7; and sectarianism 53; and social experiments 96–9; and the suffrage 136–8
Empiricism 78, 84
Enfantin, Barthélemy P. 27
Equality 101, 136–7

Colaiste Oideachais Mhuire Gan Smal Luimneach